# CARLOS LEHDER

*The Rise and Fall of a Smuggler King*

**MAFIA LIBRARY**

© Copyright 2025 - **All rights reserved.**

The content contained within this book may not be reproduced, duplicated or transmitted without direct written permission from the author or the publisher.

Under no circumstances will any blame or legal responsibility be held against the publisher, or author, for any damages, reparation, or monetary loss due to the information contained within this book, either directly or indirectly.

**Legal Notice:**

This book is copyright protected. It is only for personal use. You cannot amend, distribute, sell, use, quote or paraphrase any part, or the content within this book, without the consent of the author or publisher.

**Disclaimer Notice:**

Please note the information contained within this document is for educational and entertainment purposes only. All effort has been executed to present accurate, up to date, reliable, complete information. No warranties of any kind are declared or implied. Readers acknowledge that the author is not engaged in the rendering of legal, financial, medical or professional advice. The content within this book has been derived from various sources. Please consult a licensed professional before attempting any techniques outlined in this book.

By reading this document, the reader agrees that under no circumstances is the author responsible for any losses, direct or indirect, that are incurred as a result of the use of the information contained within this document, including, but not limited to, errors, omissions, or inaccuracies.

# TABLE OF CONTENTS

Introduction ................................................................................ 1

**Chapter 1 : Childhood And Youth Struggles** ............................... 5

   The Lehder Family ................................................................... 6

      A Conflictive Relationship ................................................... 7

      A Violent Environment ....................................................... 8

      The Violence At Home ....................................................... 9

   Life In The United States ......................................................... 9

   First Steps As A Criminal ...................................................... 11

   The Cell Mate ........................................................................ 12

**Chapter 2 : Crime School In Prison** ........................................... 13

   Meeting Jung—The Entrance To Cocaine Trafficking ............ 14

      A Profitable Business ........................................................ 16

      A New Mission ................................................................. 17

   The Initial Network ............................................................... 18

      The Medellín Cartel .......................................................... 20

   The Lehder-Jung Society ....................................................... 21

   Plan In Place .......................................................................... 22

**Chapter 3 : Operations And Strategies Of Crazy Charlie** ......... 23

   The Drug Market Before Lehder ........................................... 24

      The Cocaine Boom And The Invention Of The "Mules" ...... 26

- The Headquarters At Hacienda Nápoles ............................. 27
- Lehder Joins Escobar's Cartel ......................................... 28
  - Lehder, The Pilot .................................................... 28
- The Colombian-Bahamas-U.S. Connection ........................... 29
  - First Stop: Antigua .................................................. 30
  - Lehder Meets "The Mexican" ...................................... 32
  - The Summit ........................................................... 33
  - Lehder, The Mexican, The Boss, And El Leon ................... 33
  - The First Flights For The Medellín Cartel ....................... 34
- Norman's Cay—Crazy Charlie's Kingdom ............................ 35
  - The Journey .......................................................... 36
  - The Island's King .................................................... 38
  - The Empire ........................................................... 39
  - Lehder, The Diplomat ............................................... 40
- The End Of The Dream ................................................. 42
- Twists And Turns ....................................................... 43

## Chapter 4 : The Medellin Cartel And Its Paramilitary Force ... 45

- An Army For The Medellín Cartel ..................................... 46
  - A Kidnapping And A Vengeance .................................... 46
  - The Mas ............................................................... 47
  - The Long-Term Impact Of The Mas ................................ 49
- The Rise To The Cartel's High Ranks ................................. 50
  - The Enemies .......................................................... 52
- Emerging Differences With Escobar ................................... 53

## Chapter 5 : Lehder, The Man .................................................... 55

  A Twisted Personality ................................................................56

    Psychological Profile ..............................................................58

  A Family Man.............................................................................59

    A Don Juan .............................................................................60

  A Life Beyond Limits ..................................................................62

    Substance Abuse ....................................................................62

    Parties And Havoc ..................................................................63

  Lehder, The Politician ................................................................64

  A World For His Own................................................................66

## Chapter 6 : Lehder's Personal Objectives .................................67

  The Colombian Guerrilla And Paramilitary Forces...................68

    The Drug Trade Army ............................................................69

  The War Against The State.......................................................70

    The Extraditables ...................................................................71

  Lehder's Revolution Project......................................................73

    A Step To The Front...............................................................76

    An Escape Just On Time........................................................77

  The Crimes ................................................................................78

    An Attorney, The Justice Minister, And The Supreme Court Judge.......................................................................................79

  The Weakest Link ......................................................................82

## Chapter 7 : A Betrayal And A Fall ...............................................83

  The Political And Judicial Context In Colombia.......................84

    What Is Extradition? ...............................................................85

Colombian And The United States Interests .................................. 87
The Irreconcilable Clash With Escobar ............................................. 89
    The Incident ............................................................................. 91
Escobar's Betrayal .......................................................................... 92
The Extradition Plot ...................................................................... 94

## Chapter 8 : The Capture ............................................................ 95
The Plan Behind Lehder's Capture ................................................. 96
The Surprise Attack ........................................................................ 98
    The Capture .............................................................................. 99
An Unexpected Destination ......................................................... 101
Toward Hell ................................................................................. 102

## Chapter 9 : Trial And Sentence ............................................... 105
The Charges ................................................................................. 106
    The Indictment ....................................................................... 107
Testimonials And Evidence During The Trial ............................... 109
    More Betrayals ....................................................................... 110
Justice After All ........................................................................... 111
Never Give Up ............................................................................. 112

## Chapter 10 : Life In Prison And Afterward ............................ 113
Struggle To Recover Freedom ...................................................... 114
    Collaboration With The Authorities ...................................... 115
    Sentence Appeal ..................................................................... 117
    Sensitive Approaches ............................................................. 119
The Release ................................................................................. 120

His Life After Prison ............................................................... 121
    Back At Home ................................................................. 123
Redemption ........................................................................... 124

# Conclusion ......................................................................... 125

# References ......................................................................... 127

# INTRODUCTION

"I'm no saint, but I was disciplined and ethical. Otherwise, I wouldn't have been successful. I was never a drug addict... It was to denounce that the extradition treaty was illegal and people had to know about it" (Quesada, 2024, para. 8). These were Carlos Lehder's words in an interview in which he explained his reasons for creating the Movimiento Cívivo Latino. Carlos Lehder was many men in one: drug dealer, politician, pilot, strategist, and rebel.

In fiction or real life, criminals remain hidden or try to go unnoticed to avoid justice. Many others never admit their crimes and instead claim to be innocent to the last consequence. In this sense, Carlos Lehder wasn't a traditional outlaw. Unlike many of his partners, he was a public figure who made public declarations, some of them vindicating his actions and even assuming the role of a revolutionary.

Let's start at the beginning:

Carlos Lehder's history as a drug lord had unique characteristics. He was raised in a violent environment in the 1970s and engaged in crime, similar to other criminals. However, his childhood and adolescence shaped a complex mindset that determined his view not only of the world but also of the criminal organization he would be part of. His whole life was influenced by ideas and experiences in his early years. In the long term, these ideas and experiences made him different from his peers.

Even though we don't aim to make a profile of the criminal or engage in a sociological analysis of Lehder's life, his story and organized crime in his time require an exploration of the context. History serves us as a lens through which we can see Lehder as an actor on a stage crafted by violence and excesses.

This context begins in the familiar house and then explores how he took his first steps into crime until becoming the smuggling king. Suddenly, after reaching the peak of power, his kingdom declined. Lehder is proof that no matter how powerful a man is and how much money they gather, there is always a weak point. Usually, those who were the closest allies once are the same ones who become the worst enemies because they know exactly what the vulnerable point is, and when, and how to use it.

In his early years, he developed political ideas that fueled his plans to fight against what he considered society's enemy. Crime would be his tool, and he would join forces with the Medellín Cartel. Eventually, Lehder became the key piece of the most deadly criminal organization in Latin America. Lehder was the mastermind and the logistic strategist who enabled the Medellín Cartel to flood the U.S. market with cocaine. It is difficult to say if Lehder built the Medellín Cartel's power or if he was so powerful because of his connection with the Colombian criminal organization. In Lehder's terms, it wasn't an individual quest for wealth and power; instead, it was his idea of an anti-imperialist revolution.

This book doesn't aim to judge Lehder's ideas or actions. However, we can't overlook questions that immediately arise. Is it possible to justify crime? What is the price a society can pay for certain political ideas? Lehder shared his worldview in public interviews, during which he openly talked about his plans and motivations. These interviews are first-hand sources that allow us to hear and form opinions without speculating. His testimonials about himself provide us with raw material to know and analyze his perspective on crime and his actions.

We won't address ethical aspects or delve deep into the legal intricacies that shaped Lehder's relationship with the state. We will only describe the most relevant aspects of Lehder's life in detail, depicting all the facets that coexisted in him. It is a detached description of the life of a man who had a plan. However, you might be moved to reflect on the morality behind politics, the consequences of marginality, or the duality hidden in good and evil. People like Lehder reveal the darkest side of human nature and the fractures of society.

Now that Lehder is a free man again, we might wonder what we can learn from his story. Perhaps, this reckless figure helps us understand what lies beneath the criminal instinct and what determines its trajectory in society. We share the facts, and you will reach your conclusions.

# CHAPTER 1
## CHILDHOOD AND YOUTH STRUGGLES

Any time a criminal displays their brutality, we wonder where all that rage and violence came from. Could it be an irrational yet innate criminal instinct that has no explanation and falls beyond human control? It could also be that rage and violence are rooted in environmental factors. The human mind is a delicate puzzle in which pieces are found and placed throughout the early years of childhood. If any of those pieces is missing or forced to fit where it shouldn't go, it alters the whole picture, and personality traits drift away from what is considered normal.

If Lehder was instinctively inclined to commit crimes or if it was an undesired outcome of a turbulent childhood, we will not judge. However, it is undeniable that his childhood was far from normal. He had a complex family and was exposed to violence since he was a very young child. Even though none of this should attenuate his responsibilities for all his crimes, this background is essential to understanding how his mindset and ideological motivations were shaped.

Much of Lehder's character and ambition were crafted during childhood, and his family was very influential. His parents, particularly his father, would leave an enduring mark on his ideas:

violence as the primary valid means to reach power, to subjugate others to achieve his goals, and the cult of strong leadership were outcomes of his early education.

## **The Lehder Family**

Carlos Lehder was born on September 7, 1949, in Armenia, a city in the Quindío department in Western Colombia. It was a promising land in the heart of the country's coffee belt where Carlos' father had settled after emigrating from his homeland, Germany. His father's own story deeply influenced Carlos, and his German heritage would prove to be very beneficial many years later when Lehder was a consummate criminal and drug dealer.

Carlos's father, Klaus Wilhelm Lehder, was born and raised in Germany in the early 20th century. His life was framed by the turbulent years of World War I and the harsh living conditions of its aftermath. Germany was dragged into an economic crisis after being charged with the war costs. This crisis led many Germans to leave the country, like Wilhelm Lehder, who crossed the ocean seeking a new life. During these years, while Germany was in ruins and people had to reinvent themselves to survive, extreme right-wing ideologies emerged. Nazis and the figure of Adolf Hitler became the alternative to make Germany rebirth.

While deciding on his migration outside his country, Wilhelm Lehder was embedded in this ideological environment. From the Nazi ideological perspective, capitalism and liberalism had caused Germany's tragedy. Even though Wilhelm Lehder left the country before Hitler's arrival to power, he became a fervent admirer of his leadership and the Nazi regime.

Wilhelm Lehder arrived in Colombia in the 1940s and started a business as an engineer. Later, he started a business related to coffee production. He settled permanently in Armenia, a flourishing city in the region. He married a woman from Quindío. Her name was Helena Rivas. They had four children, including Carlos, who was the third of them.

Carlos's father bought a German immigrant's inn, which he turned into a popular hotel, the *Pensión Alemana*, usually frequented by relevant people from the local politics. He developed influential political connections with powerful people in politics and large companies. Believed to have connections with the Nazis, Wilhelm Lehder was a powerful man in Armenia and his son Carlos witnessed what money and power could get.

## A Conflictive Relationship

Carlos Lehder was raised by a high-middle-class family and received a good education. His living conditions were better compared to those of the other children in the region. His mother was devoted to her children and was very affectionate. Instead, Carlos's father was more severe and tried to instill a sense of order and authority in his children. Eventually, it had the opposite result as Carlos frequently disobeyed as a sign of rebellion.

Wilhelm tried to force his son to study and pursue a professional career and employed all types of methods, including punishments and physical aggression. Carlos, on his end, continuously resisted his father's orders. He didn't like to study and instead showed an early interest in money. Even though his father had prompted him to achieve success through hard work, Carlos was moved by the anger of his father's impositions.

## A Violent Environment

Beyond the Lehder family's house, Colombia was mired in what was called La Violencia (The Violence). While the family was the microcosm where Carlos developed a contentious personality, the social climate in Colombia prepared the breeding ground for the escalation of violence and the emergence of large-scale criminal activities.

In the late 1940s and 1950s, Colombia underwent a process of extreme violence. The conflict started with an open confrontation between the Conservative and Liberal parties, and the emergence of peasant upheavals. The clashes between the parties left over 200,000 people dead. This context favored the organization of insurgent groups that expressed a violent opposition to capitalism and the increasing coercion exerted by the Colombian government. These insurgent groups evolved into the Fuerzas Armadas Revolucionarias de Colombia, the Colombian Revolutionary Armed Forces (FARC).

The FARC played a key role in the Colombian political and social landscape for the following four decades. Carlos would become closely involved with the FARC and the armed revolutionary groups. He grew up surrounded by his father's authoritative image and admiration for Hitler, and the emergence of an extreme left-wing organization. Both opposing extremes had in common their rejection of the Western model and capitalism in the context of the Cold War. This mixture of ideals contributed to shaping Lehder's twisted perception of a revolution that blended elements of Nazism and USSR communism.

## The Violence at Home

For Carlos, violence wasn't only in the outside world but also in the jungle where peasants and revolutionaries organized the military forces to fight against the state. He had a resemblance of that violence within his house's walls.

Carlos's father wasn't only violent with his son because of his erratic behavior. He was also violent with his wife, Helena, Carlos's mother. When Carlos was still at elementary school, Wilhelm compulsorily allocated his wife to a mental health institution. He claimed that she was insane, but what he wanted was to keep her prisoner. Eventually, Helena managed to escape.

After this episode, Helena and Wilhelm divorced when Carlos was four years old, and Carlos's life took a dramatic turn. He first went to live with his father, but it didn't last long. So, Carlos was taken from his father's house and was housed in a juvenile facility. When he was 15, he moved in with his mother. Together, they left Armenia and settled in New York City.

## Life in the United States

New York in the 1960s was perceived as the panacea for Latin American immigrants. It was the promise of the American Dream, even though the dream vanished as soon as they arrived, at least for most of them. Even though life wasn't easy for immigrants, the city was fascinating. New York was a cultural hub amid an era of political turmoil. The crowded streets and the bustling life of the nights dazzled the teen from the Colombian suburbs.

By the time Carlos arrived in New York, pop art and rock 'n' roll blended in music halls, art galleries, and Broadway theaters. The Verrazzano-Narrows Bridge in 1964 symbolized the city's ongoing urban expansion and economic progress. While civil rights movements took to the streets to advocate for racial equality and social change, society evolved embedded in contradiction. It seemed to streamline endless progress, but at the same time, larger parts of the population were excluded and left behind.

Carlos was an adolescent in New York in the 1960s, and it also made a great impression on him, imprinting many aspects of his preferences and personality traits. By then, young people were captivated by the Beatles. John Lennon became one of Carlos's most admired people. Carlos was deeply moved by Lennon's public position against the Vietnam War. Like him, Carlos considered that war a result of the capitalist system's oppression.

This was also a time of the emergence of the hippie movement. This was part of the grassroots movements that protested against the Vietnam War and called for peace and free love. This eventually contributed to shaping his left-wing ideas.

This social context contrasted dramatically with Carlos's natal Colombia. For Carlos, life in New York was a revelation: Life was good, at least for some. Money and power enabled a dreamy life of leisure and pleasure but didn't suit his reality. He noticed the sharp differences between the flourishing life in New York and his homeland, struggling to adapt to the global changing market and survive political violence. Two very different flows of ideas converged to form radical thinking.

This contrast, added to the many shortages he and his mother faced as immigrants in the Big Apple, raised two feelings within Carlos: an inexplicable resentment against the northern country and its people who seemed to have everything he desired, and also, the unrestrained lust for money. Carlos himself expressed this: "'In that northern country, I fell into the temptation of the easy dollar, and I started to break the law" (Vincent, 2024, para. 13).

## **First Steps as a Criminal**

Carlos wasn't an ordinary teenager. His defiance against his father only increased after he left for New York, and increased under his mother's care. He attended school, but he didn't want to study. Instead, he preferred to read politics and philosophy books in his room. His favorites were *The Prince* by Niccolò Machiavelli, the German writer Hermann Hesse, and Hitler's *Mein Kampf*. His literary preferences showed an early interest in power and a low commitment to morality.

The interplay between the extreme right-wing ideas and the hippie movement influenced and shaped Lehder's figure as an outlaw. Being still a teenager, he engaged in petty crime. His first steps as a criminal weren't related to drugs; instead, he got involved with people who stole and smuggled cars. Even though he was a novice smuggler, he developed operations between the United States and Canada along the eastern coast. In the early 1970s, he led a broad network that smuggled stolen cars between the two countries (Cosoy, 2017).

Even though he wasn't a drug dealer at first, Carlos started consuming marijuana when he was still a teenager. It was the beginning of a long, personal, and turbulent relationship with substance abuse. In the 1960s, marijuana had flooded New York's streets.

At first, marijuana was perceived as another element of counter-culture framed in the hippie movement. Its hallucinogenic effect was a way to evade the world that was hostile and violent. It was a somewhat romanticization of substance abuse. Marijuana was consumed by youth from different social backgrounds and was in line with alcohol and tobacco as part of their leisure time.

For the underserved segments of the population, marijuana was both a symbol of resistance and a means of alienation from a society that pushed them beyond the borders. Carlos was both a young immigrant who didn't fit in that society and a rebel who sought ways to express his discontent against the system. Soon, he would visualize drugs as his weapon to fight a system he wanted to destroy.

In 1973, Carlos was sent to prison for the first time. He was caught stealing a car. After the trial, he was sent to a federal prison in Danbury, Connecticut, to serve a two-year sentence.

## The Cell Mate

While he was in prison, Carlos was housed with a criminal who would shape his path as a drug dealer. That man was the former drug trafficker George Jung. During his time in prison with Jung, Carlos learned about a millionaire businessman. Jung became the mentor who introduced him to drug dealing. Carlos discovered not only a new business model but also a new insight for his revolutionary plan to erode the system he hated.

# CHAPTER 2
## CRIME SCHOOL IN PRISON

Prisons are supposed to be places where criminals reflect on their acts and regret their crimes. However, for many, time in prison becomes a training camp. That was the case of Carlos Lehder. His first time behind bars was his opportunity to meet his mentor and first partner, a man who would show him a new "business model."

When Lehder entered prison, he was a marijuana consumer and car smuggler. After some time with Jung, he turned into a drug trafficker with a new perspective on how to amass a fortune. Lehder was greedy, and he had just been given the formula to gain money and power. Later, he would add his ingenuity and recklessness to take drug trading to unprecedented levels.

While in prison, Lehder also added a new layer to his twisted understanding of revolution. Perhaps he was genuinely moved by all the suffering around him, mainly of Latin American inmates who reached there pushed by marginality. Regardless of his true feelings, Lehder used anger and impotence to fuel his desire to fight against a system he blamed for some people's struggles.

## Meeting Jung—The Entrance to Cocaine Trafficking

Alexander Dumas' story, *Montecristo*, tells the story of two men in jail who didn't expect anything from justice or society. One was a consecrated thief who had been imprisoned for too long; the other was a man who was condemned to prison after being betrayed. They spent a lot of time together, and the first one trained him and planned a vengeance. Also, the thief revealed to him the key to finding a treasure.

It is a whimsical comparison, but we can still find some curious similitude between Montecristo and this stage of Lehder's life. The man he shared the cell with became a mentor, giving him information and ideas that weren't available elsewhere. Lehder would have probably remained a criminal, and in the environment in which he moved, he would have eventually run into the drug market. Still, his almost two years in prison served as a shortcut. Thanks to this, Lehder entered the business through the front door. Like Edmund Dantes, Lehder entered prison as an ordinary man, and after all that time with his "Abbé Faria," he came out to the world empowered and with a set of skills to bring to knees whoever he wanted.

But who was Lehder's Abbé Faria? His name was George Jung, one of the most influential drug dealers in the history of the United States, although his short career left his name overshadowed by other big fish in the business. His vision for (criminal) business put him at the front of an emerging profitable activity and started operating even before its boom. Jung had the means Lehder needed to build his empire and achieve his goals.

Jung was a student in Mississippi in the 1960s. He never finished his studies, but the blasting environment of youth rebelliousness, the student movement, and the rock 'n' roll underworld showed him people's interest in substances. According to research, before 1960, a few U.S. citizens had tried drugs. In the early 1960s, over 4 million people were assumed to have used some type of substance. By the end of the decade, that amount increased to the chilling number of 121 million Americans (*The DEA Years*, n.d.). While the authorities identified an increasingly worrying social problem, Jung saw the potential of a new niche in the market.

Jung started trading cannabis, the hallucinogenic plant with the tetrahydrocannabinol (THC) compound, from California to New England. In times when airports didn't have exhaustive and efficient security measures, he used his girlfriend, who worked as a flight attendant, to carry the drug on the planes. She simply carried it inside her luggage. Soon, Jung expanded his range of operations and started importing cannabis from Puerto Vallarta, Mexico, to Palm Springs, California. This became one of the first international links of the drug trade.

When asked about his first steps as a dealer, Jung recalls that he didn't perceive it as a crime: "I was simply supplying a need that everybody my age wanted and I wasn't looked upon as the guy in the black hat in the Sedan hanging outside the school yard" (*Interview George Jung*, n.d., para 2).

From a current perspective, drugs are a scourge that has ruined youth and entire societies, flooding the streets and social life with violence and destruction. However, to truly grasp the origins of this phenomenon, it is interesting to consider the perspective of those who contributed to building that market. For Jung, drugs were just a requested good, and he only saw it as an easy way to make a lot of money while he supplied a demand. This idea permeated Lehder and influenced his own approach to the business.

Jung conveyed that message to Lehder: Selling drugs is just giving people what they want. The system prohibited them because the power centers didn't want people to do what they wanted; instead, they wanted them to be subjugated. Drugs were a symbol of resistance, and in Lehder's mind, drugs would turn into a Trojan horse to make the system collapse.

## **A Profitable Business**

Beyond the narratives about drugs' meaning for young people, Jung shared with Lehder the impressive profits of drug dealing. By the end of the 1960s and before being caught, Jung brought 600 to 800 pounds at $20 a kilo and sold it for $300 to $350 (Bowie, 2024). As Jung kept on talking about how he ran his marijuana business and the logistics he had developed, Lehder realized destiny had put him in the same cell as this man. He was like a missing twin with the other piece of the medallion, the map to making themselves rich. Then, it was Lehder's time for a revelation.

Lehder asked Jung if he knew anything about cocaine. Jung didn't, or wanted to, try his new friend, so he told Lehder, "Why don't you tell me about it" (*Interview George Jung*, n.d., para 12). Cocaine was another popular drug in the 1960s, along with heroin and LSD. Even though marijuana was more widely consumed and the first one to take the plunge, cocaine was quickly gaining ground. Cocaine was the top dog of the grind.

Jung seemed skeptical, but then, Lehder split the number: A kilo of cocaine was sold for $60,000 in the United States, and it could be imported directly from Colombian producers for only $5,000 or $6,000 (*Interview George Jung*, n.d.). The profit margins were insane.

Lehder and Jung immediately realized they were the perfect match. Lehder had the data about where the profit was, and Jung brought the logistics to make it happen. They needed each other, and that was the beginning of a solid partnership. After that, they spent hours and hours developing a plan to reshape Jung's marijuana business to harness Lehder's knowledge and connections.

## A New Mission

During his time in prison, Lehder found more motivation for his drug-smuggling plan, motivations that had deep ideological roots. As a prisoner, he observed the terrible situations for the inmates, particularly for other immigrants like him. By 1970, the Latin American population had dramatically increased and reached 7.6 million (Gregory, n.d.). Most of them were people escaping from harsh economic living conditions or political unrest in their homelands.

Colombians, Puerto Ricans, and Cubans arrived in the U.S. cities and were often pushed to the underserved neighborhoods, and usually driven to survive by any means, which usually included petty crime. It isn't hard to understand why this was a breeding ground not only for the proliferation of drug abuse but also for a cheap and available workforce for drug trading. It wasn't unusual either that significant parts of the prison population were young Latin American immigrants.

Lehder noticed this and was deeply impressed by the harsh treatment Latin Americans received not only from the guards but also from the other inmates. He witnessed daily situations of injustice, and these people had no means to defend themselves. Lehder, influenced by left-wing ideas and the sociopolitical movement in the country, blamed U.S. imperialism and its foreign policies that condemned Latin American countries to remain underdeveloped. As part of the political climate of the time, he questioned capitalism and the social class divisions. Then, along with his dream of being rich with little effort, he committed to a new goal: He would fight against the empire, and to defeat it, he would flood U.S. streets with Colombian cocaine.

## **The Initial Network**

Like Abbé Faria and Dantes in Montecristo Island's prison planned the escape and vengeance, Lehder and Jung devoted their endless hours in the Danbury cell to outline a new business. Lehder was from Colombia and claimed to have some acquaintances closely linked to cocaine producers. Jung had the logistics: planes and port bases to move the load and introduce it into the United States.

They first focused on the network that was already working. Jung first bought marijuana in Southern California and distributed it in the trunk of his own car among colleagues in Amherst. Then, he realized it would be very easy to bring the marijuana from Mexico. Finding a connection was purely coincidental. After months of looking for someone in Mexico to start the business, Jung ran into a "young hippie girl" (in his own words) from the United States who had a Mexican boyfriend. The boyfriend became the missing piece.

This Mexican guy took Jung to a fishing boat port in Puerto Vallarta. A few miles away, it was a strategic point named Damia. They figured out how to use boats to transport the marijuana to Puerto Vallarta. Then, they took it to Damia, which served as a clandestine aircraft ramp. Jung's improvised partner got a small plane, a Cherokee 6, and landed the plane with the marijuana cargo on the beaches of California. The pilot was Jung, who had only taken a few flight lessons but dared to fly over the Pacific Ocean's waves. The system of boats and planes was key to Lehder's plans, and it would then emulate his fellow's modus operandi, but on the other coast.

Lehder visualized the plan almost immediately and became obsessed with it. He and Jung spent almost a year together in prison and used every day to think about how they would get the planes and the boats, where they would settle their base port, and where they would land their cargo. Lehder reached even further: He was already thinking about how he would launder the money he was going to earn.

The route was already decided, too. They would bring the cocaine from the Andean region in South America and use a Caribbean route to reach what would become the drug capital of the world, Miami. Meanwhile, miles away, a group of Colombian traffickers expanded their business and sought allies.

## The Medellín Cartel

In the early 1970s, Pablo Escobar, his cousin Gustavo, and the Ochoa brothers, Jorge Luis, Juan David, and Fabio, started trading marijuana and exporting it from Colombia to Ecuador first, and later, to the United States. Later, Gonzalo Rodríguez Gacha, IKEA "The Mexican," joined the organization. With Lehder, who also joined the group as the logistics strategist, the group became the Medellín cartel. They settled their headquarters in this city located in the state of Antioquia and added an office in Envigado, a smaller town near Medellín.

They started trading marijuana produced in the Andean region. They distributed the drug across Colombia and exported it to Ecuador. Nonetheless, Escobar and his partners quickly discovered that cocaine had more potential for large-scale business as its popularity increased, particularly in the United States. Escobar would focus on finding the most effective way to introduce cocaine into the North American country.

Escobar was aware of the expanding market for cocaine in the United States, particularly in New York and Miami. The business was particularly profitable due to its proximity to a major hub of cocaine production worldwide, the Andes in Peru and Bolivia. Escobar obtained the coca paste at very low prices and then refined it in his own laboratories in the Colombian jungle. The major challenge was to find a way to smuggle significant loads of cocaine into the United States.

At first, Escobar and the others used mules, a system whose invention was credited to another Colombian trafficker, Griselda

Blanco. She developed an innovative strategy to smuggle drugs by using women who carried them hidden in their underwear. Thus, the drugs passed unnoticed through the airport controls. Escobar also relied on mules to introduce his goods and later partnered with Griselda to use the distribution network she developed in Miami. By the end of the 1970s, Miami became the epicenter of the drug market due to its coastal location.

However, there was a missing piece. Escobar and associates had the goods at a convenient price and a local distribution center in the target country. Nonetheless, the business was restricted and they couldn't harness all its potential. The load of cocaine that the mules could carry was too low. They needed a more effective means of transport. That's when Lehder stepped in and brought the solution.

## **The Lehder-Jung Society**

Lehder and Jung thought about every detail. They would build a connection with the Colombian cocaine producers, the future Medellín cartel. The Lehder-Jung society they had just inaugurated had something relevant to offer, what the Medellín traffickers needed: a speed and effective means of transport that would allow them to multiply exponentially the loads of cocaine smuggled into the United States. Moreover, they wouldn't have to think about how to avoid the controls at the borders because they would create their own routes.

The base for the new plan was Jung's original network. The keys were ports for boats and aircraft ramps. Pilots, they didn't need. If Jung could pilot the Cherokee 6, Lehder would also learn to fly. However, they made a significant adjustment to Jung's network.

Instead of Puerto Vallarta on the Pacific coast of Mexico and the United States, they shifted to the Caribbean. Lehder had a groundbreaking idea: They would settle their headquarters in the islands of Antigua or the Bahamas. These islands had a strategic position for planes to recharge fuel and had direct access to the Florida peninsula.

Everything was set. They had the perfect plan to shorten and secure the routes for large loads of cocaine. Then, they only needed to capture Pablo Escobar and his men, persuade them to trade with them, and share the profit. What at first seemed to be a mere business alliance changed over time, and Lehder engaged in other Medellín cartel crimes.

## **Plan in Place**

After two years in the same prison as Jung, Lehder was a different man. He had a new purpose in his life, a partner, and a clear plan to execute. He needed only to find the Medellín cartel to offer them the master piece that would turn their criminal endeavors into an empire. As soon as he walked out of the Danbury prison, he started working on the next stage of the plan. He went after Pablo Escobar and laid the foundation stone of the Medellín cartel.

# CHAPTER 3
## OPERATIONS AND STRATEGIES OF CRAZY CHARLIE

It is commonly believed that ingenuity comes along with a bit of craziness. After all, you need to be somewhat alienated from reality to see things from perspectives that are out of sight for most common people. That's what ultimately makes a genius. Carlos Lehder was no exception to this rule.

Let's leave aside the debate about whether criminals should or shouldn't be considered geniuses if they use it to break the law and seriously harm people. Regarding men like Lehder, he certainly had skills and ideas that made him different from other traffickers. His vision of the business led him to shake the structures of regular smuggling and make it a global network that he and his group were leading.

Jung first, Escobar later, immediately realized Lehder's outstanding skills in avoiding the law and harnessing opportunities. Shortly after Escobar met Lehder, he started calling him "Crazy Charlie." A man had to be a little crazy to pilot planes loaded with cocaine into the U.S. territory and conquer a Caribbean island to use as a supply base. That's precisely what Lehder did and what turned the Medellín cartel into a global-scale enterprise.

## **The Drug Market Before Lehder**

Before the 1970s, Colombia wasn't a significant player in the international drug market, and cocaine hadn't taken center stage. Marijuana was massively produced in South America and exported to the United States and Europe in the 1950s and 1960s. Countries like Argentina, Chile, and Brazil had developed routes via Cuba, Panama City, Barcelona, and Miami. Initially, marijuana was the main product, and later, cocaine was also cultivated and processed.

Meanwhile, Colombia had a limited domestic market mainly for locally produced marijuana and coca plants. However, as the other South American countries' authorities became more concerned about the scale of drugs being trafficked, new regulations and controls emerged, forcing drug traffickers to search for new horizons. They then moved to Peru and Colombia, countries with natural conditions that were suitable for marijuana and cocaine crops. In fact, Native Americans had grown these crops for centuries, used for ritualistic purposes and also as hallucinogens. However, the reasons for drug market expansion came with political upheaval.

The evolution of a production network of illicit goods in Colombia was enabled and fueled by social unrest in the country in the late 1940s. The period was known as La Violencia (The Violence) and started as riots but developed into the assassination of politicians and protesters. Time passed, and the state couldn't find a way to reestablish peace. Instead, violent groups increased and developed new organizational levels. They became armed groups with political ideals, establishing their headquarters in rural areas.

These groups struggled for a place within the system or, better said, to replace it. In the context of the Cold War, they represented left-wing ideas and aimed to destroy capitalism and its political institutions. That struggle required economic resources because they needed to fund their military activities. They needed money to purchase weapons and ammunition, medical supplies, and other items essential for their survival in the underground.

The Revolutionary Armed Forces of Colombia (FARC), the National Liberation Army (ELN), and the People's Liberation Army (EPL) were the largest guerrilla groups that engaged in drug production and trafficking activities to supply their military efforts. Working as a parallel state, these groups controlled the production and distribution of drugs in the rural areas. They taxed and protected people who produced coca and opium, which progressively increased the amount of the loads. Meanwhile, they relied on violence to subjugate the peasants to force them to accept their rules as they established extortion and kidnapping as routine practices (Rubiano et al., 2023). This context helps us understand why the drug cartels that would emerge later found a fertile terrain and available working force to seed their business.

By the middle of the 1970s, the Colombian drug was partially targeted at the U.S. market. Meanwhile, in the North American country, drug consumption increased amid a cultural environment shaped by sociopolitical struggles. Marijuana and cocaine became increasingly popular, and the authorities were less concerned about them because the major risks were heroin and LSD. Controls and police operations were focused on those considered hard drugs, while marijuana and cocaine were classified as soft drugs.

## The Cocaine Boom and the Invention of the "Mules"

In the late 1970s, cocaine had gained terrain. It was easier to pack than other drugs, and that made it easier to hide and transport. These logistical advantages positioned cocaine as a product with a great marginal profit. It also unleashed the potential of cocaine to travel across the world.

In this context, Colombian traders seized an opportunity, considering the Andean region was historically a land of coca production. Pablo Escobar and Griselda Blanco are the most prominent figures who smuggled first marijuana and later, cocaine into the United States. With Griselda settled in Miami, the Colombian traders had a base to receive and distribute the drug across the country. In the beginning, they smuggled the drugs in suitcases, but that was too risky, and the amounts of drugs were too low to make it a profitable business.

Griselda had inaugurated an innovative way to smuggle the drug hidden behind the facade of a legal business. She used her husband's company to trade lingerie into the U.S., and used young women as models who carried the drug in the seams of their garments. Even though it meant an upgrade for the business, it was still very limited.

On the other hand, Griselda's activities raised alarms in the United States. The government had created the Drug Enforcement Administration (DEA), a specialized office to investigate and destroy drug networks of production, trading, and distribution. DEA was aware of the Colombian connection early on, and by the end of the 1970s, the name of Griselda Blanco was included in the list of wanted criminals. Thus, the recently established network needed to be updated. That was the moment when the Colombian traffickers turned to planes as the better option, and then, Lehder stepped in.

## The Headquarters at Hacienda Nápoles

During the 1970s, the United States government increased its efforts in what was labeled as the war against war. Even though marijuana seemed to be the main target, it was progressively becoming more complex to go through customs with drug loads. Simultaneously, cocaine became more popular, raising the demand and thus, the profits.

Attentive to the emerging changes in the market, Pablo Escobar included planes and helicopters in the delivery of cocaine. In 1978, he purchased Hacienda Nápoles. This ranch was only one among Escobar's many properties, but it was his favorite place where he gathered the cartel leaders, made the most relevant decisions, and served as the main headquarters.

Besides the ranch, Escobar invested in a fleet of private planes and helicopters that departed and landed at its private airstrip. Escobar started employing these planes to transport the raw material from the Andean region to the lab in the jungle, and others to take the cocaine bundles to Ecuador and then, to the United States. Along with the mansion, the artificial lake, the pools, and even a private zoo with exotic animals brought from Africa, Hacienda Nápoles had hangars to keep the planes and store the drugs.

By the end of the 1970s, Escobar had grounded his personal empire, but his endeavor wasn't free of challenges. His network was efficient, but he was a greedy man and wanted even more. Meanwhile, his competitors and enemies grew stronger as well. He needed to evolve and adapt. That's when Carlos Lehder stepped in.

## **Lehder Joins Escobar's Cartel**

After being released, Lehder devoted himself to finding a way to connect with the Colombian traffickers. They were the key to obtaining cocaine at a low price. He assumed that, being Colombian, it would be easier for him to negotiate and become involved in the business. He wasn't wrong, though what was more attractive about him was his innovative approach to logistics.

### **Lehder, the Pilot**

After leaving prison, Lehder decided to imitate his mentor, the man who had helped him outline a new path for his life. That man was George Jung, his partner from the Danbury prison. Inspired by Jung, Lehder trained to become a pilot.

Still in his 20s, Lehder enrolled in aviation classes, and within a short time, he was ready to fly small aircraft over considerably short distances. Jung used to fly single-engine planes, and Lehder knew it was enough for their purposes. He only needed space to carry some cocaine packages and fly over the Caribbean.

But that was not all. His ability to fly the plane was more than mere technical skills. He was a logistics strategist. Besides flying, he could also access some crafts with Jung's assistance. He had the flying routes to travel across the Caribbean to connect Colombia with the

Florida Peninsula, where the Colombians already had Griselda's headquarters. When Lehder explained to the Mexican who he was and what he could do, he realized that Lehder was the missing piece in Escobar's strategy. Thus, the Mexican decided to take his new friend to his partner's headquarters.

## **The Colombian-Bahamas-U.S. Connection**

Before Lehder arrived in Colombia, the problem the drug lords had was clear and concrete: how to increase the load of cocaine smuggled into the United States at a cheap cost and with fewer chances of being caught by the DEA.

Until then, Escobar and Griselda Blanco had direct operations using mules that took the drug from Colombia to the United States, particularly to Miami. When Lehder introduced Jung to Escobar, he explained how he used his own planes to transport drugs from Mexico into California through Puerto Vallarta.

By 1979, the Mexican cartels were also increasing their influence in the drug market and were Escobar's competitors. Additionally, the Medellín cartel's main base was in the Florida Peninsula, so a route on the Pacific coast was useless. That route was risky and costly, dropping the profits of the business. Escobar and other Colombian dealers also used the Mexican route. Escobar already had a network of pilots who carried the cocaine for him. However, Lehder had a superior offer.

Lehder and Jung had a better plan for the Medellín cartel. They had already established a direct connection with the Atlantic coast of the United States through the Caribbean. Lehder had thought long about this and had spent many hours looking for other options that better served the Colombians' needs. Besides planes, he figured out that drugs could also be transported in boats, for which he also devoted himself to learn how to sail boats. The next step was to design the routes to connect Colombia effectively with Florida through the Caribbean Sea.

Yet, that wasn't all. Lehder knew that the distance between Colombia and Florida was too long to be covered with vessels that could transport significant loads and go unnoticed. So, he included some stops in the voyages. He chose strategic islands in the Caribbean that would serve as stations to supply the planes and boats and store and distribute the goods.

## **First Stop: Antigua**

The first place targeted by Lehder was Antigua. This is a small Caribbean island that forms the state of Barbuda. It is located in the Lesser Antilles in the eastern Caribbean Sea, at the southern end of the Leeward Islands archipelago. By the end of the 1970s, the country was still going through a process of political independence from the British government. Thus, the institutions and armed forces were still weak. The strategic position in the Caribbean Sea and its weak frontier controls made it a perfect place for Lehder to set his base.

Lehder outlined his first move, involving his old partner from prison, George Jung. The latter had just been released from prison and planned to stay in his parents' house in Massachusetts, but his old cellmate hadn't forgotten about him. Lehder phoned him and shared his plan.

Jung had to find two young ladies who were supposed to travel to Antigua on a paid vacation. These girls would carry drugs hidden in the lining of their suitcases. These were made of plastic and fiberglass, and the drugs were placed below the lip and riveted around. It was undetectable for the screeners used at that time.

Getting through Logan Airport's control wasn't difficult for the girls. The first operation was successful, and it seemed to be fairly simple. The young ladies returned to the United States happy with their time spent on the paradisiacal island and were ready to make another trip. They were young and innocent, but they knew it was cocaine they were carrying. They may not have known precisely what that was, but it was clear it was drugs, and it was illegal. Even so, the girls were ready to join the business. That's how Lehder and Jung started their cocaine route through the Caribbean. It was similar to Escobar's method: They used mules and hid the drugs in suitcases, but the way through the Caribbean islands was innovative, and it was just the beginning. Soon, Lehder and Jung raised the pot.

Once Lehder and Jung took the first step, they had to get their own planes. They had gathered a lot of money from the drugs they sold in Antigua; they just needed to find where to buy an aircraft. According to Jung's testimony, they had many connections because both had some experience as pilots, but the options were limited because Lehder had some restrictions. So, they went to Canada, where Lehder was admitted. There, they bought their first aircraft from a pilot they knew.

Then, they refined their route map. Instead of Antigua, they sought islands closer to their destination, Miami. The same pilot who provided them with the plane gave them invaluable information: He had obtained protection from the Bahamas government. This support wasn't free; the smugglers had to pay the Bahamas authorities to look the other way on their operations. That meant they could fly in and out with cocaine loads without being disturbed, and the Bahamas were just a few miles away from the Florida Peninsula. It was perfect, and just then, Lehder and his partner were ready to approach Escobar and the Medellín cartel.

## **Lehder Meets "The Mexican"**

The first contact Lehder made with the Colombian traffickers was through a man known as the Mexican. His real name was José Rodriguez Gacha. He was known as the Mexican because he was popular for being a fan of the Mariachi, the typical Mexican musicians. In fact, Lehder got to know him at a mariachi show. Lehder was already aware of who he was: One of the principal Colombian drug lords and a partner of Pablo Escobar.

By the time Lehder met the Mexican, he had heard about Escobar, although he wasn't yet the feared boss of the mafia as he would become later. However, Escobar was leading the drug trade between Colombia and Miami. That was the man Lehder wanted to reach.

The Mexican was impressed by the young German-Colombian with crazy ideas about destroying the United States and flying their own planes to flood the American streets and houses with Colombian drugs. He sounded like a crazy, spoiled child, but the Mexican realized that the idea of the planes was, in fact, ingenious. The Mexican wanted to know more about this idealistic man with grand ambitions and fear of nothing. Then, Lehder told him about himself and why Escobar had to listen.

## The Summit

After meeting Rodriguez Gacha and sure of what he had to offer, Lehder was ready to meet Escobar. Besides the skills to fly a plane, Lehder and Jung designed new routes to shorten trips and ensure that the loads reached the destination. That was more than just a new member for Escobar's crew.

The Mexican talked to Escobar about the man he had met and his innovative ideas. Escobar had been searching for new ways to smuggle larger loads of cocaine. He had linked his business with Griselda in Miami, but the obstacles remained the same. So, Lehder seemed to be the element that would solve his logistics issues. Thus, Escobar agreed to meet with him.

With the boss's green light, the Mexican arranged the encounter with Escobar. He was impressed by Lehder. Escobar would never admit in his inner circle a person who would overshadow his power or risk his business. He anticipated that Lehder had an eccentric personality and his own motivations, but his temper, conviction, and unique skills persuaded Escobar to welcome him into his team.

## Lehder, the Mexican, the Boss, and El Leon

Despite his many crimes and flaws, Lehder had a virtue. He was a grateful and loyal man. Once he finally built his connection with Escobar and the Medellín drug lords, Lehder didn't forget the plans he had discussed with Jung for hours and hours while being imprisoned.

Lehder quickly became a key member of Escobar's team, but he didn't forget his original plan. He was behind his own business and had his own partner. So, Lehder introduced Escobar to his old prison mate, George Jung.

Some sources claim that there was a major summit between Escobar, the leader of cocaine production in Colombia, and Jung, the mastermind behind the aerial routes across Central America. These sources affirm that this summit took place in Escobar's headquarters in Hacienda Nápoles (Bowie, 2024). Other sources suggest that Jung was never in Colombia and that his link with the Medellín cartel was only through Lehder. A third version implies that Jung eventually sought a direct connection with Escobar, avoiding Lehder because his temper and ambitions made him unpredictable in a business that required the coldest mind.

Regardless of this, it is certain that Escobar met Jung before Lehder's intervention, and that was the beginning of a new scope for the Colombian drug lords. Jung and Lehder provided the planes and established their bases in the Caribbean islands. That immediately transformed into larger loads of cocaine smuggled into the United States inside simple suitcases carried by themselves in their own planes.

## **The First Flights for the Medellín Cartel**

As soon as Escobar met Lehder, he made up his mind. The Medellín cartel stopped using mules to smuggle drugs in the United States. They would rely almost solely on the planes, as Lehder suggested. Escobar used a single-prop Cessna and used Lehder's connections to transport cocaine through the Bahamas route.

The first flight took 250 kilos of cocaine that would give the traffickers a $15 million profit (Catiang, 2018). It was all produced and manufactured by the Medellín cartel, and they had finally found the way to smuggle it into the United States without depending on third parties. Lehder was already one of them. Lehder had brought his partner with him, and together, they made hundreds of flights carrying cocaine loads from Hacienda Nápoles to Miami, and coming back with the piles of dollars.

During 1978, Lehder and Jung flew back and forth with the cocaine loads almost every weekend. They took off from Hacienda Nápoles with 300 to 500 kilos of cocaine, took the package to the Bahamas, and then dropped it in the United States (Catiang, 2018). They still had the protection of the Bahamas, and Jung had his connections in Florida and the United States. Once the system was consolidated, Lehder took one step further.

## **Norman's Cay—Crazy Charlie's Kingdom**

Carlos Lehder was the link between the Medellín cartel and the Bahamas government. The deal was clear, but Lehder didn't want to depend on them. He decided that he had to own a base in the Caribbean for his illegal activities. That's when he bought his spot in the Bahamas, but first, he made some arrangements to secure his position.

The first contact with the Bahamian government was with the Minister of Tourism and Agriculture, George Smith. They met in a hotel, and after a compliment to the country, Lehder invited the minister to take a ride through Norman's Cay streets. Lehder explained he was interested in buying a property there, though he didn't give straightforward information about his true intentions.

In a second meeting, this time in a house Lehder had already bought on the island, Smith told him that the country was heading to elections. Smith was confident that Prime Minister Lynden Pindling would win, and Lehder gave him an envelope with $10,000 as a contribution for his campaign, as he explained. That was the beginning of the alliance between Lehder and the Bahamian government (Hernández, 2024).

In 1979, Carlos Lehder bought Norman's Cay with the consent of the corrupt politicians of the Bahamas. It was a small island of the Bahamas archipelago where Lehder established his base. He built a house, a hangar for his planes, a hotel, and a 3,300-foot airstrip where planes with cocaine or money landed at daylight (Green, n.d.).

Norman's Cay, owned and operated by Lehder, was 210 miles from Florida and the perfect place to refuel the planes. To keep the government's permission to operate freely, Lehder had committed to delivering $150,000 monthly, 50% more than Lehder's initial offer, through a Bahamian politician named Bannister (Hernández, 2024). This agreement with the corrupt government of the Bahamas gave Lehder a privileged position within the Medellín cartel structure. The Bahamas became and remained Escobar's main trading route for a long time, yet not the only one.

**The Journey**

Lehder developed a well-designed plan to optimize resources and secure the load and delivery. A big plane took off from Norman's Cay on Friday nights and landed in Hacienda Nápoles five or six hours later. That's the time it took to cover the almost 1,300 miles that separate the island in the Bahamas and the ranch near Medellín. Many times, that plane was flown by Crazy Charlie himself.

After landing in his partner's home, Crazy Charlie spent the night with Escobar and some of his men, usually throwing parties. But that's another chapter in Lehder's life. The next day, after recovering from a night of excesses, he flew back to the Bahamas with the loads of cocaine. Then, the drugs were put into smaller planes that took off from the coast on Sunday afternoons and flew near Florida, where they had boats that picked up the packages dropped in the sea. The operation was indetectable and unimaginable for the DEA and the U.S. government.

Nothing of this was random. Lehder was an expert and had meticulously planned each stage of the process. He knew that the DEA knew little about what happened in the Caribbean and the hundreds of little islands. He knew that Sunday afternoons had the highest peak of aerial traffic, and his planes were just minor points among dozens on the control panels. Nobody paid attention to them; nobody checked where they departed from or whether they landed anywhere or not. Thus, Lehder's planes flew near the coast and returned to the shore in Norman's Cay, going completely unnoticed.

He enjoyed the protection of the local authorities, but at some point, he stopped needing them. He had improved his method of managing it by himself. Eventually, that counted against him.

The other part of the journey was the whole way back, from the United States to Medellín, with the money instead of the drugs. Lehder was also in charge of that part. He owned a place in Florida with a fleet of Chevy Blazers. The money was packed and put inside the blazers, and taken to a workshop where the packages with the thousands of dollars were packed inside door panels that were shipped to Colombia. After a while, Lehder was ready to transport the money in his own planes as well. If he could fly in the drugs, he could fly out the money.

## **The Island's King**

Norman's Cay is a place crafted in paradise. It is a few square miles island located in the Exumas, an archipelago near Nassau. The turquoise crystalline waters bathe the golden sand, framed by palm trees and corals. It was also populated with Bahamians who didn't enthusiastically welcome Lehder.

Indeed, Norman's Cay wasn't a desert island, but that wasn't an obstacle for Lehder. He first established a relationship with the islanders. Some of them were persuaded of the benefits of having Lehder as the master on the island. The new owner promised wealth and freedom, and there was no presence of the Bahamas police or authorities. Some people accepted his presence, but many others rejected him. Lehder always had a second plan to sort out any challenge.

Lehder needed lands to establish his base and facilities, so he persuaded the islanders to sell their properties. He offered them large amounts of money so they couldn't reject the offer. He also gave them money to ignore or remain silent about his operations in the islands. Lehder also recruited people to work for him on the island. There weren't many opportunities for the people there, so for many, that was the best and easiest way to become rich. A pilot working for Lehder earned about $400,000 per flight.

For those who didn't want either to sell or become his accomplices, Lehder simply used the same method as the rest of the Medellín cartel in Colombia: violence. Lehder didn't hesitate to coercively press on people to force them to sell their properties. He also threatened them not to report his illegal activities or to take any actions that could hamper his flights and operations.

With no control of the local authorities and the community completely subjugated, Lehder was the king of the island. He made the rules and imparted justice to his will. And that meant no rules. Norman's Cay wasn't only the main operation base for the Medellín cartel flights, but also what allowed them to build an empire. It was also Lehder's playground and home to his unrestrained life of luxury and excesses.

## **The Empire**

Lehder's base in Norman's Cay and the carefully designed network that connected the island with Florida and other states on the Atlantic coast of the United States, the Medellín cartel took advantage over its competitors. The drugs were transported from a lab established in the jungle near the Venezuelan border, where the raw material brought from Bolivia was processed and packed. Escobar had around 200 local employees, either compelled or persuaded to work for them. How? Money or a bullet, the magical formula followed by the drug lords.

The planes piloted by Lehder or his pilots landed on an airstrip hidden below these people's houses, built on wheels so they could be easily moved. The pilot from the plane sent a message informing them they were coming, and the houses rolled back to release the airstrip. For years, the Colombian authorities ignored this lab and this strip, allowing Escobar and Lehder to display their operations without interference.

With the planes, Escobar and Lehder produced and traded about 5,000 kilos of cocaine a week. The production cost Escobar around $2,000, and Lehder and Jung bought it for $22,000. Then, the duo took the cocaine to the island and distributed it among several dealers with a total income of $60,000. It was a round business. For every 400 kilos of cocaine, Escobar earned $8 million and Lehder got $5 million. The cartel reached its peak in 1982 when the DC-3, DC-4, and DC-6 cargo planes flew at speeds ranging from 230 to 315 mph to carry 80 to 145 tons of cocaine. Escobar added 13 Boeing 727s to his fleet with a capacity for another 11 tons each, but he still depended on Lehder's base in Norman's Cay (Catiang, 2018).

It was a fair deal for Lehder because Escobar owned the production network while he handled the delivery. Thus, they both needed each other. At some point, Jung disagreed with his role in the partnership and separated from Lehder. Instead, Lehder continued working with Escobar and became the only leader in Norman's Cay and the flight business.

## **Lehder, the Diplomat**

While Lehder secured the routes via the Bahamas, the Cali cartel from Colombia and Mexican dealers increased their presence in the market, pressing on the Medellín cartel to refine its strategy. It was too risky to narrow the business to only one trading route, so they diversified the connections. Escobar sought connections with Central American governments that were dictatorships: Noriega in Panama, Castro in Cuba, and Ortega in Nicaragua (Hernández, 2024). Lehder made himself indispensable for these operations as well.

Lehder was a bilingual, educated man who had read a lot about politics in his youth. He also had excellent speaking skills and the ability to persuade the audience. Then, he became the Medellín cartel diplomatic representative and was involved in meetings with the dictators of the Central American countries. Moreover, Lehder also attempted to persuade the people to support the cartel, eventually recruiting many to work for them.

The strategy was similar to the one used in the Bahamas: money in exchange for the allowance to display their illegal trading activities, being undisturbed. All the parties won. The dictatorships needed money to fund their regimes, isolated in Latin America, aligned with the United States in the Cold War, and the cartel sought bases to refuel their planes on their way from the production centers to Miami.

Despite the significant trade profits through these countries, dealing with the dictators was an extra inconvenience. The Medellín cartel didn't want to rely on their will and whims. So, Lehder's island in the Bahamas remained their best option. Lehder was by far the Medellín cartel's golden boy. However, his good luck eventually ended.

## The End of the Dream

While Lehder refined his route design and the logistics to transport the cocaine and money, the DEA made improvements in its strategies to hunt them down. The agency discovered that Cessnas flying between the island and approached Florida beaches. Lehder had sorted out the coastguard by employing speedboats that sailed in international waters. There, the cocaine packages were dropped with parachutes from the planes and taken safely to the coast. Some sources affirm that the Medellín cartel even had submarines taking the cocaine from the sea to the shore (Catiang, 2018).

The DEA didn't put all the pieces together in time to stop them. Despite the efforts, Lehder successfully introduced two tons of cocaine each week, and that meant a $5 million profit for the cartel (Catiang, 2018).

Nonetheless, the DEA was confident that cocaine was being smuggled from the Bahamas. Thus, the government of the United States chose to establish a diplomatic pact with the authorities of the Bahamas. The U.S. had to make a superior offer to Lehder's.

Before the DEA approached, the Bahamian government started having differences with Lehder. The operations in Norman's Cay were gross, and while most flights were at night to avoid the U.S. radars, many other movements were at daylight. Lehder showed no shyness in displaying his business and other eccentric—and illegal—activities.

The Bahamas government had to hold a facade to cover their agreement, so on one occasion, some Colombian pilots and employees who worked for Lehder were arrested. Lehder went crazy because, from his perspective, that wasn't part of the deal. So, he took one of his planes and boxes with cash. He flew over Nassau and the surroundings and dropped money and pamphlets against the government (*Interview Carlos Toro*, n.d.). That was a turning point in the relationship between Lehder and the government.

In 1983, the Bahamian authorities received more pressure from the United States. Lehder, aware of the shift in the situation on the island, left Norman's Cay and returned to Colombia. He settled in Armenia, his old home. While he was away, the Bahamian authorities destroyed the airstrip in Norman's Cay and took control of all Lehder's properties. That was the end of Lehder's kingdom in the Caribbean and the disappearance of the Bahamian route for the Medellín cartel's cocaine.

## **Twists and Turns**

As the DEA, the Bahamas, and Colombian authorities cornered Lehder and the Medellín cartel, they increased their efforts to keep their business. Moreover, they struggled to resist the potential changes in the legal framework that would enable the extradition of Colombian convicts to the United States. That led Lehder and his partners to develop a new strategy not only within the drug market but against the Colombian state. This unleashed a tide of violence that reached every corner of Colombian society.

On the other hand, the rise of the other cartels led to an open, violent confrontation among the cartels that was known as the Cocaine Wars, in which Escobar and Lehder sought to eliminate their rivals. Besides running a profitable business based on cocaine smuggling, the Medellín cartel strengthened its other essential characteristic: the use of extreme violence to consolidate and hold full power. Lehder was also a key player in this. He was not only an effective logistics designer but also a military commander. Lehder would give the Medellín cartel the military power it needed to rule the market and put Colombia on its knees.

# CHAPTER 4

## THE MEDELLIN CARTEL AND ITS PARAMILITARY FORCE

When Carlos Lehder came out of prison, he was a new man. He had paid his debt for a crime he had committed, but he didn't use that time to reflect and reconcile himself with society. He walked out of his cell with a groundbreaking plan in his mind and a new ally. He had the formula to make himself rich and powerful, and also to conquer the empire he hated in the most subtle way.

Lehder didn't know by then that his idea would be the bedrock for developing an unprecedented large-scale drug market. With Jung's inspiration, Lehder was the missing piece for the Colombian emerging cartel to build their drug-trafficking empire. However, it didn't happen overnight; it was a process. Lehder used all his ingenuity and skills to persuade the Colombian landlords to follow his plan and made strategic moves to position himself as one of the leaders of the organization.

His fearlessness and cunning made him the right hand of the Medellín cartel's boss, Pablo Escobar. While that gave Lehder extraordinary power for some time, it would eventually lead him to ruin.

## An Army for the Medellín Cartel

By the time Lehder joined Escobar, the Medellín cartel was already formed and leading significant trading operations. Pablo Escobar and his cousin Gustavo Gaviria, the Ochoa brothers, and José Rodriguez Gacha, aka the Mexican, had a well-geared system to smuggle drugs into the United States.

Lehder's influence significantly increased not only because of his logistical approach that had leveled up the business, but mainly because of his leadership skills. He intervened during one of the Medellín cartel's hardest moments, when they were confronted by the FARC.

## A Kidnapping and a Vengeance

The concept of a cartel is mainly based on an economic criterion. A cartel is an organization that manages all the stages of production—from raw material obtention to manufacturing, distribution, and marketing of a certain product. In this case, that product was cocaine powder for consumption. However, the Medellín cartel added other layers of characteristics to that concept.

Grounded on violence, the Medellín cartel created something similar to a parallel state with its own rules and notion of justice. They had an army, with Escobar as the leader and Lehder as the second in command. The motivations were originally economic, but eventually, the group's actions were founded on political and even ideological principles, many of them fueled by Lehder.

The turning point was when the Ochoa brothers' younger sister was kidnapped. Marta Nieves Ochoa was a student of the University of

Antioquia, and on the morning of November 12, 1981, three men attacked her when she was about to get in her car. The men forced her to enter a Renault 12 and drove away. These men belonged to the guerrilla group named M-19.

The purpose of the kidnapping was to raise funds for the guerrilla groups fighting their war against capitalism and the Colombian government. They needed the money to purchase weapons, ammunition, and supplies. The kidnappers demanded a staggering ransom of $12 million from the Ochoa family, wealthy from their investments in horse trading. Unaware of his sons' murky business, the father was willing to pay the requested money so his daughter would be released. Instead, the Ochoa brothers had another plan.

## The MAS

The Ochoa brothers convoked the Medellín cartel members to a summit at the Intercontinental Hotel in Medellín on December 1, 1981. Until then, the Ochoa family had been under negotiations with the kidnappers who threatened to kill the girl if they didn't pay. On the other hand, Marta's brothers tried to gain some time while they organized a counterattack.

The summit gathered the Medellín cartel members: Pablo Escobar, his cousin, the Mexican, and Carlos Lehder. Besides them, the Ochoa brothers invited ranchers and landlords of the region who had also suffered attacks, kidnappings, robberies, or intimidation from the guerrilla groups. By then, guerrilla groups hidden in the jungle intimidated people in the rural areas. They perpetrated attacks on wealthy families, robbing their properties and deploying all sorts of strategies to gather the resources they needed. The authorities seemed to have failed to control these attacks, and people felt defenseless. This would ultimately contribute to legitimizing the Medellín cartel's justice in their own hands.

According to non-official records, the summit convoked by the Ochoa brothers gathered 223 people. They proposed to find a way to confront the guerrillas together, considering they didn't count on the state forces to control them. It is worth pointing out that none of the Medellín cartel members were recognized as criminals at this point. Escobar and the others were believed to be partners in a legal livestock trading business. They all shared a concern: what to do with the guerrilla attacks.

Lehder came up with a solution. He proposed to organize a defensive force to do what the state armed forces didn't do or failed to do. He suggested organizing paramilitary forces to fight against the guerrilla. Then, they founded the MAS, Muerte A Secuestradores (Death to the Kidnappers).

The MAS recruited 2,230 men and was funded with 446 million Colombian pesos provided by the wealthy leaders of the movement, Escobar, Lehder, and company. That money came from drug smuggling, but that was not important at that moment. The MAS stated that the money was explicitly for "rewards, executions, and equipment" (*Muerte a Secuestradores*, 2011).

The first action was to drop pamphlets on the city of Cali that expressed their mission: to hunt and execute "common kidnappers and subversive kidnappers" (*El M-19 secuestró a Martha Nieves Ochoa*, n.d., para. 8). The next step was to press on the M-19 to force them to release Martha Ochoa. In retaliation for the girl's kidnapping, the MAS kidnapped 25 people close to the perpetrators of Martha's abduction (*Muerte a Secuestradores*, 2011). One of them, one of the kidnappers' partners, was left with her hands and feet tied up in front of the *El Colombiano* newspaper with notes stuck to her body crediting the MAS for the act.

The strategy worked, and 92 days after Martha's kidnapping, the M-19 released her. It was a victory for the MAS. However, that wasn't the end of the conflict but just the initial spark. Lehder's idea would build the ground for paramilitarism and large-scale violence out of reach for the Colombian state.

## The Long-Term Impact of the MAS

Many authors agree and affirm that the birth of the MAS was the first step in consolidating paramilitary forces in Colombia. The guerrilla groups had been active for over a decade, but their organization was less structured and lacked a regular source of funds to support their activities. They were marginal. Instead, the MAS emerged as a strong paramilitary organization with a solid structure and money coming from drug trafficking to support it. They were organized like a real army.

In Lehder's mind, it all made sense. The MAS fought not only against the guerrilla, which was closer to his original political ideas but also confronted the Colombian state. Besides proving to be inefficient in controlling the guerrilla, the state had started collaborating with the United States government and negotiating the extradition of Colombian indicted people involved in drug dealing. Thus, the MAS was a rebellious group, and it didn't take long for Lehder to find his own ideological foundations for its actions.

The MAS had a lasting impact on Colombian society. It consolidated the Medellín cartel's internal organization, leaving the Ochoa brothers in debt with Escobar for saving their sister. Escobar and his men, including Lehder, gained a reputation as defenders of innocent people's lives from the guerrilla attacks. This led to people's trust and loyalty to the Medellín cartel, besides being eager to join their army to defend themselves or earn some money from the rewards for hunting guerrilla soldiers.

The conflict escalated when the MAS started operating outside Antioquia. It carried out operations in the Middle Magdalena, Meta, Arauca, Casanare, and the Valley. They became popular for the kidnappings, torture, and executions of those who were labeled as guerrilla men or were suspected of supporting them (*Muerte a Secuestradores*, 2011).

The crossfire between the MAS and the M-19 and other guerrilla groups instilled violence in society. Soon, it was difficult to separate criminals from heroes, and ordinary people didn't know who was the killer and who the victim. Fear and intimidation became the rule, which strengthened Escobar and the Medellín cartel's power. Lehder's idea became the backbone of the organization. The MAS was the armed side of the business.

## **The Rise to the Cartel's High Ranks**

At first, Lehder was accepted into the circle because he had the planes and could pilot them. However, shortly after he joined Escobar's team, Lehder became the promoter of a new modus operandi of the organization. Until then, the focus was put on obtaining the raw material—the Andean coca plant—and processing the pasta in their laboratory in the jungle. With Lehder's initiative, the organization took a step further and developed a network of violent workers that allowed them to build the cartel and seize unparalleled and unprecedented power. It can be affirmed that the Medellín cartel was formed after Lehder's initiative and became a powerful enemy for the Colombian state because of his stamp.

After the creation of the MAS, Lehder's influence over the Medellín cartel increased. Escobar was the prominent leader, but soon, Lehder became his second in command. The Ochoa brothers owed them for Martha's rescue, and thus, they also recognized Lehder's power. The man who entered as the pilot became the marshal of the team and gained relevance in all the strategic decisions for the group regarding their activities.

Lehder not only defined the routes for trading but was also one of the masterminds of the uses and misuses of violence to secure the Medellín cartel's power. Perhaps his years as a politics and war theory reader prepared him to lead a paramilitary force; maybe it was his innate impulse to become a sort of Robin Hood hero. For him, the Medellín cartel was, for some time, his means to deploy his plan to defeat the empire from within, flooding the streets of the United States with Colombian cocaine.

Lehder's performance during the operations to rescue the Ochoa brothers' little sister persuaded the rest of the team of his exceptional leadership and managerial skills. He showed his ability to organize people and allocate resources, propelling him to the top of the cartel hierarchy.

## The Enemies

As the Medellín cartel increased its power, it also gained many enemies on all sides. Their first enemy was the Colombian government. By the end of the 1970s, drug trafficking was considered one of the country's major issues. The debate revolved around the request for extradition from the United States. At first, it was labeled as a diminution of Colombian sovereignty, but as the drug cartels, particularly Escobar and Lehder's organization, became prominent, the authorities considered it as a means to press on the traffickers. Over time, it led to a dramatic bloodbath.

Lehder became one of the most fervent advocates for open war against the state to ensure they wouldn't be extradited to the United States. His desperate attempts to avoid the extradition agreement from happening led him to make terrible decisions that cost hundreds of lives, including innocent citizens, police officers, soldiers, and members of the government.

Another enemy of the Medellín cartel was its counterpart in Cali. It was another cartel that fought to take the center of the business. The violence unleashed by Lehder set the pace for the competition between the two organizations. The increasing power of the cartel would have consequences for Escobar and, as a ripple effect, on Lehder. Eventually, a complex spiderweb of treason and impossible alliances led to one's fall and the other's capture.

There was an external factor that became Lehder's personal enemy: the DEA. The DEA had been created during the Nixon administration to enhance the U.S. government's efforts to control drug activities. During the 1970s, the DEA had improved its strategies and resources to track and capture drug traffickers and had many of the Colombian drug lords on its list of most wanted criminals. Lehder was one of them. From Lehder's perspective, the DEA was just another element of the U.S. imperialism that couldn't stand South Americans leading profitable businesses. His resistance against the DEA and its plan to establish extradition became another edge of his ideological struggle against the country he hated.

Aligned with these ideas, Lehder would assume a complex position within the Medellín cartel regarding yet another enemy, the guerrilla forces. As explained, Lehder founded the MAS to confront these left-wing groups, but over time, guerrilla groups sought financial support from the cartel. Escobar agreed to cooperate with them in exchange for military support and diverse illegal services, but eventually, he didn't engage with them. Escobar had his own war and his own methods. Instead, Lehder sympathized with certain left-wing ideas inspired in his youth by the hippie movement and the social upheaval. Thus, he had a different approach. That would be a turning point in his relationship with the boss.

## **Emerging Differences With Escobar**

Lehder quickly gained influence within the organization he contributed to consolidating. He had leadership skills, was fearless, and pursued greater goals, making him ambitious and unscrupulous. Lehder gave the Medellín cartel the army they needed to seize informal power and created the war that would involve society in a turmoil of violence. The chaos served the cartel's objectives.

While Lehder created the chaos for the cartel to rule, he also built the routes for the cocaine to fly directly from Colombia to Florida. Thanks to Lehder, the business scaled at unprecedented levels in terms of the amount of smuggled drugs and astonishing profits. Escobar was the boss, the leader of the cartel, and enjoyed the personal loyalty of the other members, but it was Lehder, the man with the vision and the hand on the control panel. Lehder's entrance to the Medellín cartel not only stands out for the creation of the MAS and the inauguration of terror as the organization's policy, but he also created a world network of smuggling and crime.

# CHAPTER 5
## LEHDER, THE MAN

Carlos Lehder was the type of man who knew how to make himself indispensable and had the virtue to make it both an advantage and a threat. His intelligence and endless resources to enhance the business machinery took him to the leading roles of the Medellín cartel. Nonetheless, his temper and singular personality made the others feel suspicious about him. What made Crazy Charlie so contradictory and conflicting?

When analyzing Lehder's role in the Medellín cartel and, particularly, his expulsion from it, Lehder's personality and behavior become central elements to understand why. At some point, it was his lifestyle and decisions that made him the first Colombian drug lord to be extradited to the United States. He could persuade anyone to do what he wanted, even Escobar. He could design a trading route that fooled the U.S. security system. However, he constantly fell victim to himself. He failed to master his own impulses.

Behind the genius—for the good or the evil—there is always a man. No matter how great the ideals they pursue or the excelling skills that make them different from the ordinary, in the end, they are moved by simple, mundane wishes: selfish, uncontrolled appetites that blur even the most cold and calculating minds.

Behind the thirst for money and opulence lay the greed for power, and along with the inclination to break the rules, came the struggles to recognize when crossing the limits was off the plan. Yet, Lehder was a man who was moved by deep beliefs, and within his logic, he sought to remain true to them. While lost in excesses, he tried to have a family, perhaps the one he was deprived of when he was a child.

That was Lehder. The same paths that took him to the peak dragged him to the shadows. Even though Carlos Lehder is still alive at the time of this publication, this section refers to his personality and profile when he was Norman's Cay's king and one of the Medellín cartel's leaders. His essence might not have changed over time, but life eventually tempers people's character. As years passed, his personality traits probably remained but became less exposed through his acts and behaviors. For now, let's focus on Carlos Lehder as Crazy Charlie.

## **A Twisted Personality**

A quick search on the web about Carlos Lehder would provide a curious, long list of adjectives that describe his personality. In simple terms, those who knew him thought he was simply mad. That's why they called him "Crazy Charlie." He made decisions as if he didn't consider the consequences, had no sense of good or wrong (or had a very personal perspective on that), and acted impulsively more than he listened to advice.

According to the diverse testimonials of people who worked for the Medellín cartel or Lehder himself, he owned a complex and intense personality that blended charisma and egomania, fueled by an extraordinary intelligence and fanaticism driven by his readings as a teenager. He described himself as "an armed, rational, good-hearted pacifist, who shows mercy to his enemies" (Quesada, 2024, para. 4). Nonetheless, researchers who interviewed people who knew Lehder and crossed hid path by chance affirm that he was impulsive and violent, feared even by his criminal partners.

His charisma helped him establish social bonds quickly and in any context. While in jail, he captivated Jung, persuaded the Mexican and Escobar to do business with him, and made many people love him in the Bahamas. Even though he relied on violence, the truth is that a lot of people saw him as a benefactor. There was something in his way of addressing his audience that overpowered them. As he inspired loyalty in many, he also had a tone and style that intimidated his enemies. Escobar, for instance, had opposing feelings toward him, sometimes of trust and camaraderie, and on other occasions of suspicion.

Lehder was also a fanatic, which is both a virtue and a source of danger. Unlike most criminals, driven only by greed and ambition, Lehder had deep ideological motivations. Raised in a German filo-Nazi home, he had developed admiration for Hitler as a political leader. He was also moved by the hippie movement and the ideals of the 1960s and 1970s in the United States and Latin America. Only in his mind could he find connections between these two systems of ideas, but he did, and they were the foundations for every choice he made.

The other main characteristics were his egocentrism and megalomania. He bought an island for himself and performed like its king. He believed he was carrying out the revolution that would tear down the United States, its empire, and capitalism. He didn't think he was selling an illegal product to become rich; it was his personal fight against the system.

## **Psychological Profile**

Specialized profilers used Carl Jung's theory of psychological types and the Myers-Briggs Type Indicator (MBTI). Within this theoretical framework, Carlos Lehder has been cataloged as ESTP: extraverted, sensing, thinking, perceiving by specialized profilers. According to this label, Lehder was a "fearless trailblazer, master of the moment, street-smart thinker, and reality-focused problem solver" (*Carlos Lehder Personality*, 2023, para 1).

According to this profile, Lehder displayed cognitive functions such as extraverted sensing and introverted thinking. As an extraverted sensing person, he was aware of everything happening in his surroundings and strongly wanted to engage with the physical world. That is a clue to understand why he fell into excesses. Also, this trait implies that the person is practical and hands-on, making decisions based on experience rather than abstract ideas. No wonder he ended up buying an island to improve their trading routes.

On the other hand, being an introverted thinker means that he analyzed all the information in depth before taking action, and sought internal coherence between his ideas and actions. This trait results in a person with a strong problem-solving capacity. In Carlos Lehder, both combined traits gave him unique skills to process lots of information and turn his conclusions into actionable strategies to solve complex problems. Also, these cognitive functions gave him highly developed interpersonal skills and a unique communicative style (*Carlos Lehder Personality*, 2023).

Experts indicate that Lehder was motivated by an overwhelming desire for achievement and a need to validate his self-worth. His greatest fear was to fail, not achieve success, or not be cherished by others. That would explain why he always went the extra mile to please Escobar, accomplish greater goals, and bring grandiloquent ideas.

Besides these character traits, Lehder was a man of multiple facets. One of them was his love for his family, a love that was damaged in many ways by his uncontrolled way of life.

## **A Family Man**

In 1983, Lehder left his island in the Bahamas to avoid being captured by the DEA and came back to his homeland. He settled in Armenia, where his parents used to live. By the time he reached there, Lehder had a daughter he recognized and carried his surname, though some sources suggest he had another daughter born in the Bahamas.

The information about Lehder's relationships and children is scarce and confusing. Most of what is known comes from his memories and some interviews. It is known that he had one daughter who carries his surname. Her name is Mónica Lehder, and her mother was a woman from Medellín. Her name was Liliana García, and Lehder met while he still lived in the Bahamas. They had a brief relationship that didn't last because she wanted to start a family, but

Lehder was still too busy as the pilot and logistics strategist of the cartel.

However, when Liliana got pregnant, Lehder accepted her decision to give birth to the child. Since she didn't want to remain on the island or return to Colombia, Lehder gave her money to travel and settle in Spain. She went to live in Malaga, where Mónica was born and raised. According to Mónica's testimonials, neither she nor her mother inherited any money or property belonging to Lehder. Despite this, Mónica has always devoted words of love and care to her father in public declarations (Redacción Nación, 2025).

## **A Don Juan**

As a ray of his charisma, Lehder was a seducer. Lehder loved women as much as money and didn't spare resources to obtain more and more of them. He was known for his parties with strippers and prostitutes, but he was also a romantic, so he had many relationships that were important to him, as he revealed in his memoirs, the book *Vida y Muerte del Cartel de Medellín* (*Life and Death of the Medellín Cartel*).

Lehder met love for the first time when he was a teenager and lived in the United States. Her name was Melody, and she came from a wealthy family in New York. According to Lehder's testimony, Melody left her family and joined him during his first years as an outlaw, before becoming a drug lord. They lived together in Los Angeles and Miami, but when his issues with the law increased, she returned to her home in New York.

When established in Norman's Cay, Lehder had a woman he called Chocolata (Chocolate). She was a blonde woman who was by his side during his years as the king of the island and the leader of the Medellín cartel's operations. When the DEA and the Bahamian government cornered Lehder, he sent Chocolata and her daughter to Colombia, where they would be safe. It is uncertain if the girl was Lehder's daughter. Though he called her "My Bahamian child," he didn't recognize her as his daughter, and she didn't have his surname (Lancheros, 2025).

Also in Norman's Cay, Lehder met his only daughter's mother, Mónica, whom he called Ojitos ("little eyes"). Their relationship was brief, and the woman left the island.

In Medellín, Lehder engaged in a relationship with the woman he considered the love of his life. Her name was Lulú, and she was his companion during the darkest moments in Lehder's life, when he had lost power within the cartel and was overwhelmed by his addiction. In his words, he loved her; it was mutual, and she was devoted to caring for him. The relationship ended when she went to live on her family's ranch in Armenia to start medical and psychological treatment for her addiction to drugs.

Lehder's magnetism also attracted Yolanda, the woman who stood by his side when he was a fugitive. Lehder had settled in a ranch in Llanos Orientales to put him out of sight of his many enemies, already alone by that time. Yolanda was only 19 years old, the daughter of a couple who worked for Lehder. Yolanda was with him until Lehder was invited to Hacienda Nápoles. She realized it wasn't a safe place for her and separated from Lehder.

Esperanza and Pestañas ("eyelashes") were two frugal yet passionate stories in Lehder's life. Esperanza was a girl Lehder used to know before moving to the U.S. She sent him a letter and moved in with him for a while to his ranch in Llanos Orientales. She left the place because she got infected with malaria. Pestañas met Lehder through Griselda Blanco, the Cocaine Godmother. She was also involved in the drug business, and after the brief affair with Lehder, she was killed outside a disco in Medellín.

These stories overlap rather than following a chronological order. They are a depiction of how intensely and anarchically Lehder lived his life.

## A Life Beyond Limits

Don't blend work with pleasure, business with personal life. That rule applies to almost every field, and this murky drug trading wasn't an exception. Lehder didn't adhere to that rule. Perhaps because his megalomaniac personality led him to believe he would have things under control. He was wrong.

As his profile defines him, Lehder had a broad understanding of his environment, motivating him to interact with it as much as possible. He was a passionate man who seemed to squeeze life. He didn't want to leave anything undone or anything untried. That was Lehder, and driven by his passion and desires, he crossed every limit.

### Substance Abuse

Drug dealers are supposed to trade drugs and become rich from it; they are not supposed to use them. No drug dealer ignores the impact of drugs on people's lives. They know drugs blur the mind and make them weaker, and business people with such power can't afford a blurred mind or weakness. Escobar, for instance, would smoke a joint while throwing the parties, but never went any further.

Instead, Carlos Lehder became a drug consumer, and soon, it became an issue for himself and the cartel. Lehder started smoking marijuana when he was a teenager while living in the United States. Later, he added cocaine and other substances. He didn't only use drugs when he was in one of his outrageous parties; he used them in everyday life, even when he came to meet Escobar and the other cartel members to make relevant decisions.

Lehder had no control and turned into an addict. That became a problem for Escobar because he became unpredictable in a context requiring the coldest mind. Crazy Charlie had taken the wildest road.

**Parties and Havoc**

Along with wealth and power comes the desire to showcase it. Other drug lords like Escobar and Griselda Blanco were famous for the parties they offered. They used their mansions and properties to provide their guests with all types of pleasures: food, drinks, shows with famous people from the entertainment industry, women, sex, and drugs. Lehder didn't fall behind them and had his own parties. The only significant difference was that while the others used the parties to strengthen their control, Lehder was a victim of himself. He used the parties to feed his lust and recklessness.

In Norman's Cay, Lehder had his house, the hangar for the planes, the storehouse for the drugs, and the airstrip, but it wasn't only an operational base. He also had a hotel, a restaurant, guest houses, and a marina. The island was his kingdom. He didn't need Escobar's permission and was out of the boss's control, so he didn't repress any impulse.

The result was outrageous events with all sorts of excesses that didn't go unnoticed by the local authorities, and particularly the neighbors. The initial arrangement with the Bahamian government was to use the island to refuel the planes, as part of the route to the United States, but the situation was getting out of control, and, after all, they had to preserve the facade of a serious state. People around Lehder's properties were aware of his illegal activities, but the scandal reached far beyond his walls.

Lehder invited close friends to his parties, people he wanted to get involved in the business, potential enemies and allies, and just anyone. The parties weren't part of a strategy or with a deliberate purpose. It was just an expression of his unlimited hedonism and megalomania.

## **Lehder, the Politician**

The scandals of the parties were an extra ingredient that complicated Lehder's relationship with the Bahamian authorities. Lehder had crossed the line, and along with the undisguised flight operations, the Bahamian government took away the protection in 1983. He had to escape and return to Colombia, where he lived in different places while he sought a new place within the cartel.

Lehder settled in his family's property, "La Posada Alemana" (The German Inn) in El Quindío for some time. The inn served as a local hotel in the rural area and also as his personal residence, where he continued operating as a Medellín cartel member. There, he continued living in opulence and eccentricity, and of course, surrounded by excesses. On one occasion, Lehder hired a renowned Colombian artist and ordered him to create a statue of John Lennon to be placed in his property. Lehder was a fan of The Beatles and wanted to honor John Lennon's memory. He had been murdered in New York in 1980. The statue was odd: Lennon was naked, with three bullet holes on his chest showing the shots that killed him, a guitar in his right hand, and the word "love" on his genitals—Carlos Lehder's style tribute.

Besides promoting local tourist activity and contributing to culture in a singular way, Lehder continued traveling to Hacienda Nápoles to participate in the cartel's meetings. However, being a drug dealer wasn't his only "job." Lehder revived his old ideals and got involved in local politics. He had his own media, the ROC 102.4 FM radio station, and the *Quindío Libre* (*Free Quindío*), a local circulation newspaper. He had always cultivated political ideas and revolutionary objectives. He used these media to spread his ideas against the United States and denounced the North American country's imperialist policies. He painted himself as a hero who fought against what he described as disguised colonialism. Additionally, the Colombian government had advanced in negotiations with the United States to approve the extradition agreement. Lehder fiercely resisted extradition and was determined to make his personal quest a national issue.

Besides disseminating his ideas, Lehder also actively sought access to the local legislature. He joined and supported the ultra-nationalist party Movimiento Cívico Latino (National Latin Civic Movement), for which he provided financial support. In his own terms, the party was meant to "denounce that the extradition treaty was illegal and people had to know about it" (Quesada, 2024, para. 8). Perhaps Lehder believed he would reach the national political landscape; instead, he added issues to his already conflictuous relationship with the cartel, particularly with the boss.

## A World for His Own

Business partnerships are complex, particularly when dramatically different interests and objectives drive the parties. We can say Lehder was a team player. From the first moment, he teamed up with Jung and remained loyal to that relationship even when Lehder became a powerful man in the Medellín Cartel. Then, as Escobar's second in command and aware of his influence in the business, he respected the boss's authority. Lehder could have had a separate business, but instead, he agreed to be one piece in the major gear.

Unfortunately for Lehder, the people he related to had different perspectives. Lehder was helpful for some time, but his personality, personal issues, and political motivations became an unbridgeable gap between Lehder and Escobar and the rest of the cartel. At one point, Lehder's uncontrolled lifestyle and the alliances he sought for himself went against the group's interest. The cartel members started pressing Escobar to drive Lehder out of the group. However, Escobar would find other, more personal reasons to get rid of Crazy Charlie.

# CHAPTER 6
## LEHDER'S PERSONAL OBJECTIVES

After escaping from Norman's Cay, Lehder came back to Colombia. Despite having lost the main operational base, he was still a relevant member of the cartel. He played a key role as a diplomat in the cartel's relationship with the dictatorship that allowed them to use their airports to transport the drugs, and was also one of the leaders and strategists of the armed wing of the organization. His struggles with substance abuse shadowed his power, but moreover, it was a shift in Lehder's priorities: He put his own objectives before the cartel's interests.

Lehder rediscovered his old political goals in his land and his family's property. He assumed the character of the revolutionary. Before joining the cartel, Lehder felt drugs were a means to fight against the United States. As the extradition treaty between the North American country and Colombia advanced, Lehder took that idea to the extreme. Instead of only corrupting society with drugs, he decided to take more direct action. He started an open war against the Colombian government, and that led to a bloodbath against the Colombian people.

## The Colombian Guerrilla and Paramilitary Forces

In December 1981, the M-19, a Colombian guerrilla group, kidnapped the Ochoa brothers' younger sister and claimed a millionaire ransom. Instead of paying the money, Carlos Lehder promoted the organization of the MAS (Muerte A Secuestradores, which means Death to the Kidnappers, as we learned in Chapter 4). Initially, the main target of the paramilitary violent actions was the Colombian guerrilla. The MAS had popular support. The guerrilla terrorized landlords and people in the rural areas because they constantly attacked them, searching for resources to support their plans.

The situation worsened as the Colombian authorities stared in passivity and helplessness. People stopped believing that the law and the legitimate power could stop the guerrillas and defend them. So, they supported this group of criminals who seemed to have the sources to fill the space the state failed to occupy. Ranchers, business people, and common people collaborated with the Medellín cartel, and hundreds of people responded to Lehder's invitation to join them. It was the birth of paramilitary forces in Colombia to oppose the already active guerrilla.

At some point, even the government seemed to benefit from the MAS because they were more effective in eliminating the guerrilla that threatened and terrorized citizens. In a way, the Colombian government allowed the MAS to grow stronger and chose to look the other way because the ultimate outcome was desirable. The MAS was fighting the guerrilla, which the legitimate armed forces couldn't deal with, and it was—or seemed to be—costless for the state. However, the government and society would pay a high price in the long term.

## **The Drug Trade Army**

It is difficult to know if everyone who supported or joined the Medellín cartel was aware of the criminal activities. Lehder and the others held an image of wealthy business people in the horse and livestock businesses. However, in a context of increasing violence, people cared less about the background of those who were effectively capable of defending them. Moreover, the Medellín cartel had no issues in recruiting people to join their illegal army. They relied on fear—fear of the guerrilla groups and fear of the cartel. But that wasn't the only strategy.

In the Bahamas, Lehder had deployed typical political strategies to earn people's support. He showed himself as a man concerned about people's needs, brought progress to the forgotten side of the island, and cared about building close relationships with the neighbors. He used to give them money and offer them protection. Similarly, in Colombia, the Medellín cartel—particularly Escobar but also Lehder—depicted the image of benefactors. They provided people with public services and houses, and supplied what the state failed to. In a context of poverty and marginality, the Medellín cartel offered them jobs and an opportunity to improve their living conditions. They paid a high price, but the limits between good and evil blur when people are helpless.

The cartel recruited young people—men as hitmen and girls as escorts—in exchange for significant amounts of money, which they wouldn't get by any other means. Thus, the Medellín cartel didn't take long to grow a large army that responded to the personal leadership of Escobar and Lehder. This led to an unprecedented scaling of violence that the Medellín cartel used to pressure the government. They declared war on the Colombian government, and as they felt more cornered, they increased the cruelty and number of crimes, first targeting the public armed forces and high-ranking politicians, and then the common people.

Even though Escobar was the boss, Lehder had his own people because he was a charismatic leader. Living on his ranch, Lehder had a lot of people working for him. He used his media to reach local people and instill his ideas. People approached him just searching for money, while some others may have been driven by the illusion of a revolution, or after the promise of a better life. The fact is that within the Medellín cartel, Lehder was a hindrance to Escobar, who had no intentions of sharing the power. However, Escobar needed Lehder's abilities, connections, resources, and recklessness to confront the pressure of the Colombian army and the United States.

## **The War Against the State**

Between the late 1970s and early 1980s, the Medellín cartel played a cat and mouse game with the Colombian authorities and the DEA. The United States had identified the Colombian drug lords as the main ones responsible for smuggling cocaine into the country and worked intensely to achieve an extradition agreement with the Colombian government. In exchange, they provided Colombia with weapons and intelligence services to trace the Medellín cartel, among other key players in the drug business.

The Medellín cartel used this collaboration between the Colombian authorities and the United States to turn the issue into a nationalist quest. From Lehder and Escobar's perspective, extradition was an intrusion on Colombian autonomy and a violation of Colombian citizens' rights. Of course, the truth was that they didn't want to be judged in the United States, where their power had no weight. In Colombia, they found a way to pressure judges, police, army chiefs, and politicians to influence legislation to benefit themselves.

Lehder and the Medellín cartel had used money to buy powerful people's will, and if money wasn't enough, they relied on violence. Like other drug lords, they used the "plata o plomo" (money or bullet) system. They didn't hesitate in executing or threatening government officials, policemen, judges, prosecutors, journalists, and anyone who could take any action against their criminal business.

## The Extraditables

As the extradition agreement progressed, the Medellín cartel leaders thought the resistance should be better organized. The Colombian state and the United States had declared war on drugs, and they prepared to resist. SO, Carlos Lehder promoted the foundation of a new organization: the Extraditables.

In 1986, Carlos Lehder went to Bogotá to have an interview with the lawyer Pablo Salah Villamizar, an old friend who was well aware of his criminal record. The meeting was two blocks away from the Colombian Palace of Justice. Lehder wanted Salah to confirm the rumors in the press about the extradition agreement. Lehder and the other members of the cartel believed that it was a trick displayed by the Colombian authorities to discourage them, but that it was practically impossible to implement.

To Lehder's surprise, Salah handed him a folder with some documents. The extradition agreement was ready, and the only missing step was the approval of the Colombian Congress. According to Lehder's memories, Salah gave him a copy of the document that was still confidential and made him promise to never reveal where he had obtained it, a promise that ultimately Lehder didn't keep.

Salah recommended a colleague to represent Lehder and advised him in legal matters. His name was Valencia. Lehder realized that the situation was complex and decided to search for support from public opinion instead of the law. He asked Valencia to organize a press conference where he could explain the implications of such an agreement. Lehder aimed to clarify the extent of the agreement, should it receive Congressional approval: The president would gain the authority to extradite any Colombian citizen sought by the U.S. legal system, subjecting them to American laws for any offenses committed (Lehder, n.d.).

Valencia discouraged Lehder's idea. The press conference would be a mistake; instead, he suggested paying for an advertisement in one of the newspapers with a larger circulation across the country, *El Tiempo* (*The Time*). The advertisement would spread the message to alert public opinion about the threat to Colombian sovereignty. It should have a powerful impact.

When the lawyer asked Lehder about the signature for the advertisement, Lehder refused to use his name. He believed that he wasn't popular enough to impress the audience. Then, he said that the emissaries should be "the extraditable."

That was the birth of the new paramilitary organization, this time aimed not at fighting against the guerrilla but the Colombian state. Lehder paid a considerable amount of U.S. dollars to the journalist who published the official declaration by the Extraditables. That declaration stated that they preferred a tomb in Colombia rather than a prison in the United States. It became the Extraditables' *leitmotive*.

Lehder went back to Medellín and brought a copy of the document. When he explained to Escobar what it meant, the boss was infuriated. They decided that it was time to play hard on the Colombian authorities. If they were ready to deliver Colombian citizens to the United States, they would give the government and anyone who supported them no peace.

## **Lehder's Revolution Project**

Besides their fight on the streets as the Extraditables, the Medellín cartel also tried to play in the political arena. Pablo Escobar ran for a seat in the Colombian Congress. He aimed to gain influence in Congress and impede the endorsement of the extradition agreement. On his end, Carlos Lehder joined the Latino National party, though its participation was in local legislatures.

Some sources suggest that Lehder founded the party and it represented his neo-Nazi ideas. The party's ideas and proposals were a mixture of nationalist vindications and extreme civism, with some elements that can be linked with Nazism. The symbols were

Jorge Eliecer Gaitán—a liberal leader—Simón Bolivar—a leader of the Latin American revolution—and a map of Quindío, the Colombian department. Lehder proposed that the Hispanic people were a superior race that would conquer the United States and displace those he called "the Yankees."

It is possible that Lehder aimed to spread his fascist ideas and confront both the left-wing guerrilla and the liberal state, but his primary motivation was to ban the extradition agreement. He engaged in political rallies, gathering popular support to help Escobar reach Parliament. The party achieved three seats, and Lehder became popular for his speeches against extradition, although that adventure didn't last long. When the political strategy failed, Lehder put all his efforts into armed fighting.

In the mid-1980s, Colombia was a bloodbath. The government fought on two sides. On one side, there were the guerrilla groups that, after many executions, decided to stop firing and agreed on a sort of truce. However, dozens of guerrilla leaders were captured or killed, and the guerrilla accused the government of breaking the tacit pact. Thus, they returned to committing terrorist attacks, and the inner war intensified.

On the other hand, the Colombian government had commitments with the United States that they should honor. Thus, they doubled the efforts to chase the drug lords with Escobar and Lehder at the top of the list. The DEA was also behind them. Meanwhile, Lehder's relationship with Escobar also weakened. Lehder wasn't the owner of the Caribbean route anymore, and his weight in the political negotiations with the Latin American dictators wasn't exclusive. Lehder was still a key piece because he was completely mad and would do anything to prevent the extradition agreement from becoming a reality. He became obsessed with that. However, the problem with Lehder was that his idealism and personal involvement with the matters blurred his reason in times when the coldest mind was needed. He was a time bomb and became progressively more isolated within the cartel.

As violence rose, the Medellín cartel became divided. Some of the members wanted to negotiate with the government. Their idea was to surrender but demand that the government desist from the extradition agreement. Lehder, on the contrary, thought it was impossible to negotiate with the authorities because they would not respect a deal with them. Lehder proposed to take the conflict to the last consequences. The Extraditables had to put the Colombian state on its knees, and Escobar eventually stayed on his side.

This confrontation and his leadership in the conflict gained Lehder many diverse enemies: the DEA, guerrilla groups, the Colombian authorities, people of the Cali cartel, and some of his own partners in the Medellín cartel. Even though Escobar was on his side about this, Lehder progressively lost power within the organization. As his profile rose, he felt more cornered until he had no choice but to become a fugitive.

Lehder left Colombia and hid in Cuba, Mexico, Brazil, and Peru, but returned to his country. He returned to fight in his territory and continued making mistakes that persuaded Escobar that he wasn't a man the cartel could rely on. He was lost in excesses, and his personal objectives seemed to be more important than the cartel. Lehder would not listen to the others' opinions and concerns and dared to make decisions on his own, decisions with consequences for the whole group.

Every time the cartel struck the state or people, the reaction of the government was more severe. The war heated up, and the state was simply unbeatable; no matter how many hitmen and collaborators the cartel recruited, there would always be more police officers and soldiers because the state is a major organization. Lehder believed he could defeat the Colombian state, not only the president in office or the military chief in charge. He thought he could dismantle all national institutions to prevent himself or other criminals from being taken to the United States.

## **A Step to the Front**

Back in Colombia, Lehder settled in Hacienda Airapua. It was a luxurious ranch located in the department of Meta, in the Eastern Flats. By then, Carlos Lehder was one of the most wanted men by the DEA and the Colombian public forces.

At first, Lehder acted as if he were immune. He even offered interviews in his residence and invited journalists with their cameras. He didn't hide his face or change his name for those interviews. He felt ready to speak to the people as Carlos Lehder, a revolutionary who used violence to fight against what he believed to be unfair. In those interviews, he spoke about his political ideas, his opposition to Western capitalism, and how he aimed to destroy it. He also spoke about the Extraditables and their mission to defend Colombian citizens' rights to be judged and condemned or released according to their nation's legislation, not a foreign jury.

At some point, Lehder had reasons to assume he was at no risk of being captured or sent to prison. Even though crimes accumulated by dozens, and public opinion as well as the authorities knew that it was them, that the Extraditables were the Medellín cartel, the fact was that there was no evidence to prove it. The Medellín cartel had always sustained a facade of legal businesses, and Escobar was a popular face in the national political realm. Lehder thought becoming more popular would ignite people's support, so he appeared on Colombians' televisions and newspapers.

Besides not having evidence against them because they had the money to cover their tracks and eliminate any potential witnesses, the Medellín cartel also used public exposure to increase the pressure on the government. Once people knew them and what they did, what they fought for, and how far they could reach to preserve their freedom, people had two choices: either to support them or to fear them.

Lehder's idea was to develop a public image similar to a sort of Colombian Robin Hood. They were accused of trafficking drugs and killing people, but for the people, they offered money, job opportunities, and public services, as well as protection. That protection was a response to the violence they created in the first place, but for people, those were the options.

## **An Escape Just On Time**

Lehder's public appearances made him a preferred target for the DEA and the police, who were working closely to hunt the cartel down. In April 1985, the DEA displayed an extensive intelligence operation, and they found out he was hiding in the Eastern Flats.

Escobar had his own people doing intelligence as well, and was able to inform Lehder to the last minute that the cops were approaching.

Lehder was in his residence with his men, who guarded the perimeter. As soon as he received Escobar's warning, Lehder barely had time to pick up drugs, weapons, and money that could incriminate him. However, the cops arrived faster than expected, and Lehder had to hurry to avoid being captured.

When the police arrived, Hacienda Airapua and the neighboring one, El Pescador (also known as La Gaitana) were empty. None of Lehder's men were found, but Lehder left $1.6 million in the rush. Even in those days, it was quite a fortune, but that was just petty cash for the Medellín cartel's assets.

## **The Crimes**

After losing the base in the Bahamas, the situation dramatically changed. It was a sign that the DEA was closer. If Lehder and company thought extradition was only a legal technicality, they realized it was a feasible possibility after watching the DEA knocking on their doors. Lehder lost his compass, the Medellín cartel lost its balance, and even the boss, Escobar, was upset. They had already lost Tranquilandia, the hidden lab in the jungle. Then, the authorities dismantled Lehder's property on the island and soon found him on his private ranch. No matter how many people they intimidated by fear or money, they had undercover people among them. The Medellín cartel fell into despair.

Desperate people make desperate decisions. When talking about criminals, that can only mean they took their cruelty to the limit. As they feared more the possibility of extradition, and understood that the government was eager to deliver them to the United States if they were caught, they saw as the only option to deepen the pressure on the government by terrorizing society. The terrorist attacks, kidnappings, and executions were typical resources used by the drug cartels, but what the Extraditables started in Colombia had no precedent.

The primary targets were public servants, police chiefs, lawyers, judges, and prosecutors. The cartel aimed to send a strong message: They would kill whoever was needed to compel the authorities to reject the agreement. Every time the mutilated bodies appeared, they left signs or made public declarations, taking responsibility for the crimes. While some Medellín members insisted on surrendering to appease the government, Lehder was the first to persist in his plan of pressing harder. His message was only one: They could kill anyone and everyone until Colombia stepped back from the extradition agreement.

## An Attorney, the Justice Minister, and the Supreme Court Judge

The Medellín cartel committed countless crimes, some against people who betrayed them, some against others who tried to steal from them, and many others against their enemies—other cartel members and drug leaders. However, as the extradition issue advanced, Escobar and Lehder made a shift and started targeting the highest ranks in the Colombian government.

They used a brutal and rudimentary strategy. After weeks of intelligence on their victim, they displayed an attack mainly carried out by hitmen on motorbikes. Once they learned the victim's routine, the routes they followed, their schedule, and the people who surrounded them, the hitmen were ready.

The first significant crime framed in the extradition matter was in April 1984. One of the most astonishing crimes was against the Justice Minister, Rodrigo Lara Bonilla. The minister had started an open and strong campaign against drug trafficking and supported the extradition agreement, defying the increasing threats he received both in his office and at his home (*Justice Minister Slain in Bogotá*, 1984).

On the night of April 30, 1984, the minister was traveling in his limousine with his bodyguards following it in a jeep at a short distance. At some point, the limousine slowed down because of a traffic jam. That was when a motorbike with two riders approached and opened fire at Lara Bonilla, who was inside his car. The bodyguards shot at the aggressors, and one of them was killed, but it was too late—Lara Bonilla received three shots in the head and three in his chest and throat. The limousine driver immediately took him to the hospital, but he died 10 minutes later.

The initial hypothesis was that the crime could have been a left-wing guerrilla attack, but one of the aggressors confessed. He said the Medellín Cartel had paid him $20,000 to kill the minister (*Justice Minister Slain in Bogotá*, 1984). While many sources point out Lehder as the mastermind behind this crime, the criminal insisted on denying his responsibility.

Lehder testified that it was all Escobar's idea and planning. Lehder sustains that Escobar killed Lara Bonilla as a personal affront and not as part of the cartel's strategy against the government. In fact, many years later, Lehder reflected on his own actions and claimed that he always tried to save his own skin rather than fighting the system. In a public declaration, he was asked about Lara Bonilla's murder. After some seconds in silence, he said: "I did not participate in any assassination or plot. I have chosen to defend my life in circumstances in which it was life or death. But never against the Colombian government" (Quesada, 2024, para. 6).

That wasn't the only crime, but it was the most resounding. It reached the headlines of all national and international newspapers and TV programs. Everyone talked about the Extraditables. Then, crimes continued. On January 25, 1985, the cartel abducted the Colombian attorney Carlos Hoyos.

That day, the hitmen followed Hoyos's car on a road. When the vehicle was near Medelin's new airport, the hitmen approached, fired at the guards, and took Hoyos from the car. Another car driven by another hitman reached, and they forced the attorney to enter the trunk. Then, they simply left. Hoyos was wounded during the attack. Later, his body was found along another road. He had been executed with a short-distance shot.

Between 1985 and 1987, while the extradition agreement was discussed in Congress and finally enacted, kidnappings and executions continued. One of the most resounding crimes was the murder of the Supreme Court Justice Hernando Baquero in July 1986, and many other police officers, judges, and other officials.

Even though the Extraditables publicly credited themselves for the crimes, neither Lehder nor any of the cartel members were convicted or judged for them. The extradition agreement was finally enacted, but the crimes remained unpunished.

## **The Weakest Link**

Between late 1984 and the beginning of 1987, the Medellín cartel evolved into a powerful and dangerous criminal organization in Colombia. Led by Lehder, the Extraditable emerged as the new armed wing of the cartel, determined to force the government to abandon the efforts to achieve the extradition agreement with the United States.

Throughout these years, Lehder was Escobar's marshal. However, despite the many roles Lehder still had within the organization, Escobar believed he was too crazy and didn't trust him anymore. Lehder had his own projects and vision of the cartel and was his own boss. All these were incompatible with Escobar's notion of power. Lehder was indomitable and followed his own rules. That turned out to be unbearable for Escobar.

Lehder knew the cartel inside out and was Escobar's first accomplice not only in the drug business but also in the many crimes the cartel committed. Nonetheless, Lehder's personality, excesses, and some unexpected events—a byproduct of all the rest—led the relationship to a point of no return.

# CHAPTER 7
## A BETRAYAL AND A FALL

It's been said that too many cooks spoil the broth. And two leaders were too much for the Medellín cartel, at least from Escobar's perspective. Lehder had turned a dangerous man for himself and the organization, and Escobar wasn't willing to be at any risk. Lehder had money and people who supported and followed his leadership directly, but he was out of control. In part, because Lehder's issues with the substance had deprived him of a sound mind and good sense. On the other hand, Lehder had gone crazy in the face of the possibility of being extradited to the United States.

The Extraditables had said in their public declaration that they preferred a tomb in Colombia rather than a jail in the United States. For the others, it was meant to persuade the government of their determination to go to the last consequences; Lehder, instead, had taken this statement too seriously.

Lehder had invited journalists to his ranch and offered interviews, and had spoken freely about drugs. He had linked drug trafficking with his crazy idea of a revolution. The Extraditables were meant to resist the government's decision to enact the extradition agreement, but no revolution was behind. It was just the Medellín cartel's strategy to save their skin. Lehder had his own interpretation of the situation and the cartel's goals. Escobar would not let him rule or hamper everyone's business.

The man who had the Medellín cartel in his hands and ruled the main traffic route in the Caribbean was given away by the same men he helped build a millionaire business. The man who had the genius to weave a complex network of planes, airstrips, and smuggling routes lost control of the security lines that were just around him. The man of the complex negotiations and the risky diplomatic relationships failed to see the infiltrated spies he had in his own troops and house. It was his temper and uncontrolled style of life that cornered Lehder. He was surrounded by the authorities and left alone by those who used to be his allies. But it was a betrayal that ultimately led to his end as the smuggler king.

## **The Political and Judicial Context in Colombia**

Why was Lehder so scared of being extradited? What were the differences between being judged in Colombia and in the United States? He was going to end up behind bars anyway.

That's partly true, not only for the legal implications but also for the other parallel strategies that the cartel members planned to display if they were caught in their country. In Colombia, the Medellín cartel members were local. They had devoted years and tons of money to persuade and threaten people. If they were sent to prison, they were sure to have the means to reverse their situation. Neither Escobar nor the others wanted to spend some time in jail, but if they had to, they were certain to access the right connections to do what they pleased. If they were taken to the United States, they wouldn't be able to pay judges and prosecutors to negotiate the sentence, or would at least find it more difficult to bribe the guards to get what they wanted.

This doesn't mean that Colombian laws were more flexible or benign than the United States system. It wasn't about Colombians being more permeable to corruption than North Americans. It was a matter of preparation. Escobar and the Medellín cartel had full power in their territory, but it had been built over the years. It was impossible to recreate it in the United States, where they were already wanted, where there was more competition, and where the state had far more resources to hold a war against drugs.

## **What Is Extradition?**

Extradition is the act of one country handing over a person to another country for legal action or punishment due to crimes committed within the first country's legal system. It is applied to serious crimes typically defined by both implicated jurisdictions, meaning that both countries consider it a crime and require a mutual agreement. One country accepts that its citizens are judged and condemned for a crime committed in both countries, but under the other state's law, even if that worsens the convicted's situation.

Many societies have utilized extradition since antiquity, and it is not free of controversy. A state is defined as a legal system that determines the rights and duties of its citizens. It is a prerogative for citizens and an attribute of the state's sovereignty. However, when crimes imply far-reaching consequences, extradition becomes a necessary tool to fight against them. That is the case of crimes related to drug smuggling and other types of organized crimes.

The Medellín cartel took raw material from Peru and Bolivia, stored it for some time or displaced it through Ecuador, manufactured it in Colombia, used the Bahamas, Mexico, Nicaragua, Panama, and Cuba to transport it, and introduced it in the United States to finally distribute it in the main cities streets. Where was the crime of drug trafficking committed? There is only one answer: in all those countries. However, not every country is open to extradition treaties.

It isn't just about legal aspects. From a legal perspective, it makes sense to collaborate in fighting organized crime, but politics is usually intertwined in the negotiations. For local powers, allowing a foreign country to intervene in judicial procedures can be seen as a sign of weakness or damage to sovereignty. Even though extradition is only requested when crimes are severe, citizens in general may sense that they are vulnerable and could potentially be judged without the corresponding guarantees stated in their constitution or set of laws.

Another aspect not related to justice but politics is the use of extradition as part of a larger negotiation. For instance, countries would feel compelled to accept an extraction agreement in exchange for other benefits such as financial or military support. These edges were used as arguments by Lehder to speak against extradition. While he attempted to manipulate public opinion against extradition, he continued to find ways to remain hidden and avoid the authorities.

## Colombian and the United States Interests

Extradition was a hot topic in both countries. In the United States, President Reagan expanded the reach of the war on drugs. Incarcerations for non-violent drug offenses and public campaigns aimed to shift public opinion. In 1986, Congress passed the Anti-Drug Abuse Act and allocated $1.7 billion on anti-drug procedures. Despite the legal and economic efforts, the government seemed to fail in stopping access to drugs on the streets. In this sense, Lehder was winning: They were flooding the U.S. streets with cocaine, and the government couldn't stop them.

The DEA was quite aware of the origins and routes followed by the cocaine that was traded in the United States. They knew they were Colombian and thus, the extradition agreement was urgently needed. It wasn't enough that the Colombian government hunted them down with their support; the United States had to prove to its citizens that its laws and security forces could defeat drugs. They needed the public image of Colombian traffickers being brought to the United States, and judged and condemned by the United States laws. It was a war on drugs, but it had a strong political implication as well.

In Colombia, extradition was a very delicate matter. The agreement was signed in 1980, but it took seven years to be effectively enacted. In 1986, the treaty was amended, and drug smuggling was included as a crime that could involve extradition. The Colombia-United States agreement stipulated that the three branches of the government—Executive, Legislative, and Judiciary—were involved in the procedures. The last steps were to be taken by the Supreme Court. One of the main obstacles, besides the threat coming from the cartel and the pressure through violence, was that there were other operating issues.

Colombia's courts had over 4,000 cases of violent aggression on the judges' desks, most of which were never solved. Society perceived the judicial power as inefficient, incompetent, bureaucratic, and corrupt. It was difficult to gain support for extradition. Moreover, the delay in approving extradition between 1980 and 1986 was marked by political skirmishes between the presidential candidates. For the Colombian president in office, extradition meant violating the nation's sovereignty and accepting being overpowered by the United States. This was even more complex considering the conflict with the left-wing guerrillas that had heated up in those years. Only by 1985 did the guerrillas accept a cease-fire and negotiate with the government.

The murder of Lara Bonilla was the last straw. Contrary to the Extraditables' expectations, that attack didn't force them to retreat from the agreement but persuaded them to sign it. After the murder and the confession of the perpetrator, the Colombian government decided that Colombia had had enough. It was clear that their efforts weren't enough to stop the Extraditables, the cartels, and violence. Thus, the government approved extradition (InSight Crime, 2025).

In the Congress opening session, President Belisario Betancur addressed that despite his initial reluctance regarding extradition, he considered that the country claimed justice. Alleging that drug crimes had no boundaries, the extradition agreement was formally enacted. During the following years, Colombia would extradite over 20 Colombian citizens accused of drug trafficking (Nagle, 1991).

The beginning of extradition from Colombia to the United States unleashed an even more extreme wave of violence in the country. The Extraditables doubled the stakes and increased the number of casualties, including police officers and judges. However, Escobar was a smart man and didn't rely on only one strategy. He decided to play other cards, in part to keep the government's hand off his cartel—or at least, his inner circle—but what was even more important, to get rid of a disturbing element within his troop. What at first was a major threat turned into Escobar's resource to remove the unwanted member: Lehder.

## **The Irreconcilable Clash With Escobar**

It is hard to describe personal relationships within criminal organizations. Is it possible to talk about loyalty or friendship among criminals? They had common businesses and shared interests, but that forced them simultaneously to trust each other while looking over their shoulders. They knew too much about each other, including their vulnerabilities.

Lehder entered the circle of what would become the Medellín cartel after other members, some of whom were Escobar's relatives. Lehder arrived as an outsider and soon became part of Escobar's close circle, but that didn't make him his friend or a second leader of the cartel. Lehder's power came from his usefulness, reckless commitment, and Escobar's approval. When those attributes vanished, Lehder became a loose end.

For a long time, Escobar needed Lehder. He would probably have never been able to build the Medellín cartel's empire without Lehder's planes and political abilities to negotiate with the Latin

American dictators. However, when Lehder's structure collapsed and he succumbed to drugs himself, his preponderant role within the cartel clashed. Escobar had too many issues to attend to, and Lehder had become more of a load than a resource. With his personal struggles with drugs and other excesses, Lehder was uncontrollable and a time bomb.

When the cartel formed the Extraditables, Lehder returned to the center of the scene. Perhaps because he suspected Escobar was thinking about getting rid of him, Lehder played his card well with the extradition document copy and the public declaration. Lehder had proven once more that the cartel needed him. For a while, he was right. Escobar needed Lehder to continue his war against the Colombian state, particularly considering that some of the other members were part of the negotiation. Lehder was the only one willing to continue with the open attacks.

The enactment of the extradition agreement after the murder of Lara Bonilla made Lehder look as the responsible for pushing the government to take the action they were trying to prevent. It matters little if it was Lehder's idea or if he was the real mastermind behind the attack; it turned out to be a huge mistake. And Escobar would never take responsibility for errors in front of the other cartel members. After all, it was Lehder who insisted on this crime and others against the highest magistrates at every summit of the cartel members. If the idea had been Escobar's, it ultimately was instilled by Crazy Charlie. Lehder would pay the price.

## The Incident

Despite his cruelty, Escobar was a leader, and as a leader, he was cautious with his decisions against his people. He had developed an image of a fair leader whose actions were based on justice and collective purpose rather than on vengeance or personal interest. That was his method to grow and sustain his men's loyalty. He couldn't just kill Lehder or make him disappear. He would wait for the perfect occasion.

Escobar was confident that Lehder would eventually give him many opportunities to take action. One night, Escobar threw a party in Hacienda Nápoles to thank his henchmen for their performance. As usual, the party offered alcohol, women, and drugs. Escobar used these parties to make his men feel rewarded and forge camaraderie among them. While the others became intoxicated, he prudently observed and controlled everything, remaining sober or only having a marijuana cigar.

However, that party had a hidden purpose. Besides the henchmen who guarded his properties and his hitmen, Escobar had invited Carlos Lehder. It wasn't a party meant for the cartel leaders. Escobar planned different events for them. It wasn't coincidental that Lehder was there that night.

During the party, Lehder didn't behave like the boss. He drank and ingested cocaine, losing control over himself. At one moment, intoxicated and out of his mind, Lehder engaged with a woman. There was a skirmish with one of Escobar's closest hitmen, a man named Rollo. The circumstances of the dispute are confusing because they were only known through testimonials retrieved from a few men there. Apparently, Rollo was with this woman whom Lehder was interested in.

At 2 a.m., most guests were gone or asleep. Lehder was also already sleeping, exhausted from everything he had taken. Rollo was one of the few still awake and had the terrible idea of hammering on Lehder's door to ask him for more cocaine. Everyone knew that Lehder shouldn't be disturbed under any circumstances because he had a terrible temper. That night was even worse because Lehder was furious with Rollo for messing around with the woman he had been flirting with. Lehder, furious, opened the door, took his gun, and shot Rollo. Escobar heard the shooting and came downstairs. He went crazy when he found Rollo's body in a pool of blood (*The Midnight Murder*, n.d.). However, that was the sort of event Escobar was waiting for.

With Rollo dead, the party was over. When Lehder saw that Escobar treated him like the other men and was visibly upset, he realized that his time in the Medellín cartel had ended, just like the party. He just needed to figure out how Escobar planned to get rid of him. Certainly, Escobar had the resources to eliminate him in a hundred different ways, but Escobar's plan was completely unexpected.

## **Escobar's Betrayal**

Besides the armed attacks, the terrorist attacks, and the fear they spread, the cartel also displayed many diplomatic lines to remain untouched by justice. They had political connections with the different players in the Colombian system.

Lehder, for instance, was in charge of the negotiations with the left-wing guerrilla. According to his memories, he met Jacobo Arenas and Manuel Marulanda Vélez, alias Tirofijo, the leaders of the FARC guerrilla movement. They made an arrangement. Lehder settled in a ranch in Vichada and gave him in exchange 10% of the profit he made with the drug he trafficked, coming from that place. The cartel benefited from this arrangement because the money was used in the FARC war against the state. That kept the government busy, and the public forces were divided as they had to fight on several fronts, and public opinion was distracted by the war against the guerrilla.

This alliance was also a matter of concern for Escobar. Even though Lehder was on the antipodes of the FARC, they were military forces that Lehder could eventually use. Lehder had never taken any action that could be labeled as betrayal, but he was impulsive and violent. Escobar was cautious about him.

On the other side, Escobar had his own political alliances and murky strategies. When he entered politics, he attempted to join the Liberal Party but was publicly rejected by the candidates. Besides taking it as a personal offense, Escobar shifted the strategy. He urged a plan to make it seem the Liberal Party received funds from drug trafficking. The Liberal Party used extradition as one of its campaign promises. Thus, this connection with the Medellín cartel dirtied the party's public image and its candidate. According to Lehder, Gonzalez Gacha, on his end, made his own financial contribution to the Conservative Party, which eventually won the presidential elections.

In sum, while in front of public opinion, the state was in open war with the drug cartels, behind the scenes, envelopes with dirty money came and went. The Medellín cartel had many connections with the people in office of the different administrations during the 1980s. Escobar had no scruples in using any of his resources as long as they served his own interests. When the situation with Lehder reached a point of no return and before Lehder decided to use his own weapons against the cartel, Escobar decided to play the political card, even if that meant betraying one of his men.

## The Extradition Plot

When Lehder left Hacienda Nápoles that night of the incident, he was sure that his life was in danger. He became paranoid, thinking that Escobar was behind his back. In a sense, he was making exact calculations despite the effect of the substances he had taken. However, he was wrong about Escobar's plan.

Lehder imagined Escobar would hunt him down as he had done with so many enemies and traitors in the past. Lehder believed he would be shot while sleeping or having a bomb under his car seat. Not even in his worst nightmares would he have imagined that his final destination would be a prison in the United States. Even more unexpected was that he would be delivered by his own partner in crime. How could Escobar give Lehder away without compromising his own situation? Lehder couldn't guess that his delivery was part of Escobar's safeguard to avoid extradition himself.

# CHAPTER 8
## THE CAPTURE

Lehder was a clever man. When he got up that morning in Hacienda Nápoles after killing Escobar's hitman, he understood there was no room for him in the cartel. The boss wasn't there to offer him breakfast, and didn't show up when he was leaving. The bond with Escobar was broken forever. It was time for Lehder to find innovative ways to serve the cartel and revitalize his leadership; it was time for him to disappear.

Despite having quite a fortune, it wasn't easy for Lehder to leave without a trace. He could hide for a while, but he had too many enemies: the DEA, other cartels, the Colombian government, and then, Pablo Escobar added to the list.

Lehder retreated to his property in the middle of the jungle and prepared to resist. He knew that the Colombian authorities had found the Medellín cartel in the jungle and they had knocked on his own door twice, taking millions of cash and tons of cocaine. The Colombian army had cutting-edge technology delivered by the United States, and the military was training special forces to track traffickers. Moreover, authorities found a way to play under their own rules and persuaded people in the neighboring rural communities to collaborate by providing information about the traffickers.

For Lehder, things were even worse because Escobar provided him with the intelligence support to spot the Colombian forces approaching. At that point, Lehder had to reorganize his defensive rings, be cautious with the communication, and prepare his personal army. He was certain that he should fear Escobar's rage more than the authorities.

## **The Plan Behind Lehder's Capture**

The fateful party in Hacienda Nápoles took place in 1987. Escobar didn't talk with Lehder the next morning but sent his emissary. Lehder received the boss's order to hide in the jungle where nobody would find him. Escobar promised Lehder that he still could count on his protection. However, Lehder didn't believe it. He was certain that Escobar had decided to kill him, and that was just a trick so he wouldn't suspect. But did Escobar have reasons to kill Lehder?

In fact, if Escobar only wanted to get rid of him, he could have just shot at him after the party, or sent one of his hitmen with Lehder when he was going back home. However, he chose not to. Probably, Escobar didn't have enough reasons to kill Lehder. He had to make a firm decision because Lehder had just killed one of his closest men in his own house, during a party he had organized for his henchmen. It would seriously damage Escobar's image among the men who were loyal to him.

For people who are risking their lives, money may not be enough. It never happened, but what if all those men attempted to mutiny, or simply left? The cartel never had issues recruiting new people to serve as hitmen, but times were convulsed. The police had shot down many of them, and the struggles with justice were increasing. It wasn't a timely occasion to renew the troop. On the other hand, Lehder had his own army, which was made up of people who were loyal to him. They could take retaliation—or at least, attempt to—if Escobar killed Lehder, and the Medellín cartel couldn't afford a new front. They were already at war with the state, the DEA, and the Cali cartel.

Escobar needed a clean operation. His close circle had to know he had pushed away Lehder to protect the cartel and his men. Meanwhile, Lehder and his people had to believe it was an external enemy, not Escobar. It wasn't easy, but Escobar figured out a plan.

Lehder's temper, political motivations, and excesses that drove him crazy had turned him into a stone in Escobar's shoes. Escobar had a personal impulse to make him disappear, but he realized that Lehder was more valuable alive than dead. If Lehder just died, Escobar didn't win anything. And he was a businessman. He always won something. So, Escobar turned to some of his old connections in the political landscape.

Lehder's role had fallen within the cartel, but for the authorities, he was still the second in command of the Medellín cartel. The DEA and the Colombian government wanted him. Escobar saw it as an opportunity. The open war against the Colombian state didn't have the expected results. Since the extradition agreement was enacted, Colombians accused of drug crimes were sent to the United States, no matter how many people the cartel killed in the streets. Escobar's strategy seemed to be failing. So, Lehder appeared as a trading piece for a potential truce.

## **The Surprise Attack**

Suspicious or not, Lehder did what Escobar ordered. He had been a refugee from justice for years, so he had hideouts in the jungle where he thought nobody could find him. He took his weapons with him, his army, and his lover. Despite taking some precautions, Lehder couldn't help being himself. He couldn't just give up on drugs and a life of excesses, so parties and guests were still frequent in his hideout.

It is unknown if anyone in his close circle revealed information to the authorities. According to different sources, including Lehder's testimony, Escobar himself provided the information not only about the hideout but also about the night the Colombian armed forces launched the operation to capture him.

Mark Bowden, the author of the book *Killing Pablo*, affirms Escobar betrayed Lehder, and Lehder confirms it in his biography. In his book, Lehder recalls that while waiting for his trial, his lawyer had access to certain documentation confirming this suspicion. Lehder tells (Torrado, 2024):

Among the hundreds of papers that the Attorney General's Office was delivering to my lawyers before the start of my trial, one document was [included] by mistake. In this way, my lawyer learned of secret official information. Even though several lines of the text were crossed out with black marker in the document, it was possible to see that Pablo Escobar was the person who had handed Carlos Lehder over to the Medellín Police (para. 20).

When this information was revealed, Lehder had no further reason to lie about it. If he ever had the intention to blame Escobar for all his crimes, it made no sense because Escobar had already been killed in 1993 while attempting to escape from the police. It is believed that Escobar approached the authorities seeking a deal to protect himself. At first, he believed the United States and the Colombian government were more interested in the FARC than in drug lords, but he was wrong. He was willing to reveal what he knew about the FARC, but when he found out that Lehder was a better prospect, he negotiated information about his hideout. He delivered Lehder in exchange for an amnesty for his crimes (Cosoy, 2017).

## **The Capture**

If Escobar didn't reveal the details of Lehder's hideout, it could have been any person living nearby. The local people were aware of what happened at Lehder's ranch. They saw the vans and cars and the strange arrival of armed people, women, and all types of strange behaviors. They heard the noises of the parties and the shooting. Everyone around knew that Lehder was a drug trafficker. By then, the police had found a way to break the cycle of loyalty and found relevant information about the location.

Regardless of who delivered the information, the police chose the perfect moment to display the capture operation. Lehder was in the middle of a party, probably high as usual after having alcohol and drugs, and also his men were alienated. Lehder had learned from

Escobar and had different security concentric rings. From the outside to the inside, each of them was supposed to prevent the next one if they saw any suspicious movement or received any alert through their satellite radios. Escobar, who had his eyes and ears within the police and Colombian army, used to send alert messages when any movement could mean an operation. Nonetheless, that night, there was no alert.

It was February 4, 1987. William Lemus, the marshal of a town named Rionegro, was warned about a party at a ranch named Berracal. A group of police officers, led by Lemus, approached the ranch in the middle of the night. The thickness of the vegetation and the darkness covered them, and Lehder's guards didn't notice any movement. As they had been told, everyone was engaged in the party. When the police assaulted the property, they were all unprepared and didn't engage in any armed resistance.

After a couple of shots and a man wounded in his buttocks, Lemus and his men were in control of the situation. The men of the party quickly surrender. One of those men was Carlos Lehder, one of the most wanted criminals.

After the successful capture of the drug lord and his men, Lemus declared to the press that it was a simple routine operation in response to the local people's report of disturbing episodes on the ranch. According to his testimony, he had no idea who they would find there. He may have received the order to proceed without too much detail, or it was just a trick to avoid the ins and outs of how they truly found Lehder.

## **An Unexpected Destination**

When Lehder saw the police entering his house, his first reaction, besides showing an incredible surprise, was to attempt to grab his rifle and defend himself. Soon, he realized it was useless because his men weren't ready to fire, and the police officers were too many for him alone.

Used to always getting away with it, Lehder opted to let them do it. Lemus told him he was under arrest. Lehder just smiled and cursed them for interrupting his party. He yelled that they didn't know what they were doing and threatened the police with retaliation when all that was over. Lehder was very certain that nothing was going to happen. Escobar would appear to buy his freedom, or a cartel squad would come to the rescue. And if that didn't happen, justice would never find the evidence to prove he was guilty. It was just a matter of time.

From his ranch, he was taken to another place near Guarne in Antioquia. There, he was delivered to U.S. Drug Enforcement Administration agents. Eleven hours later, Lehder was put in a plane heading to Miami. Even when he was taken to the plane, Lehder was smiling. He didn't believe that he was being extradited. He had just been arrested! How could everything move so fast in a country where bureaucracy ruled?

Lehder didn't know it, but the Colombian president had signed his extradition order in May 1984 (Cosoy, 2017). They were waiting for that moment to show the world that one of the leaders of the Medellín cartel had been captured and extradited.

When Lehder realized that extradition was happening for real, he made one last attempt to save himself. He offered to the U.S. officers: "Listen, I can help you capture Pablo Escobar… You can put me under the security of the Colombian army, and I can find Pablo Escobar for you" (Rennie, 2025, para. 29). It was too late.

## **Toward Hell**

The impossible had happened. When Lehder wrote "better a grave in Colombia than a prison in the United States," he never truly believed it would happen. In fact, he hardly believed when he was on the plane. He knew he had lost Escobar's support but held his hope to the last minute. Escobar should be scared to be the next.

What if Lehder gave him away? What if he used all the information he had to trade it for his freedom? Lehder was certain that those ideas were crossing Escobar's mind and the cartel would intervene to rescue him from the gringos. However, nothing happened. The plane that transported him took him to the United States, where he was informed that he was under U.S. law. He would be judged and punished in the country he had sworn to destroy. He was defeated.

Lehder was the trophy the United States needed to show the citizens that all the efforts and budget allocated for the DEA and anti-drugs operation were finally paying off. For the Colombian authorities, it was proof that the extradition agreement wasn't against the country's autonomy, but it was contributing to dismantling the most dangerous drug cartel. Of course, the public opinion didn't know that the Cali cartel had its deals with the government, and that the authorities had negotiated with Escobar himself to have at least one important drug trafficker convicted to justify the agreement.

In a sense, Lehder was the scapegoat for a system that continued to fail in its war against organized crime. Some time later, Lehder discovered that his old partner in crime had traded him for a truce. Lehder was the payment for Escobar's freedom, at least for a while. Lehder's extradition was the beginning of a new chapter in the global fight against drug trafficking, although in the long term, it would prove that it wasn't enough.

# CHAPTER 9
## TRIAL AND SENTENCE

February 1987 was the beginning of a new chapter in the history of organized crime, at least regarding extradition. Lehder was a big fish, and his arrest caught the attention of the global media. It was propaganda for the DEA, for the United States, and also for the Colombian government. After Lehder, hundreds of Colombians indicted for drug offenses were extradited to the United States, although the others didn't attract the flashes of the cameras and didn't reach the headlines.

In sum, extradition worked as a symptom of collaboration among countries, but in practice, the amounts of cocaine in the streets didn't decrease. Nonetheless, this doesn't mean that the criminals affected by extradition didn't have to pay for their crimes, either in the United States or Colombia. It should serve as an exemplary punishment, but the results weren't as expected. The activities of the Medellín cartel continued, and violence even escalated once more. Lehder's extradition was taken as a victory of the government and Escobar, even if he delivered his partner, insisted on covering Colombia in a blood bath. The execution of politicians and judges seemed not to be enough, so the new strategy was to openly attack

Colombian society through terrorist attacks. Hundreds of innocent people died in the streets.

Distant from all that, Lehder faced his own struggle, a different one. Under arrest and alone, Lehder was resourceless. He tried to use his old methods, but they didn't work in the United States. He was a wanted man, but not for what he could offer to the other Medellín cartel members' capture. He was valuable only in jail. Both governments only sought his image on a trial, receiving an exemplary sentence, and walking to his cell, where he would spend the rest of his life. Lehder in prison meant the triumph of justice over crime, of good over evil. However, Lehder had his own version of his actions, of justice, and of good, so he would never stop fighting for his freedom.

## **The Charges**

The plane that left Antioquia on February 5, 1987, landed in Jacksonville, Florida, a few hours later. Even when they arrived and stepped off the plane, Lehder didn't credit his own eyes. It couldn't be true. It had to be Escobar's job. It had to be Escobar acting out an extradition, maybe to get rid of or threaten him. But still, the news was on every TV screen: Carlos Lehder had been extradited from Colombia to the United States.

Lehder was taken to a maximum security prison in Atlanta while the prosecutor prepared the case. Then, he was taken to a federal prison in Jacksonville, Florida, when the trial was held. He was considered a highly dangerous prisoner, so the trial required a special security operation.

## The Indictment

Lehder's indictment was finally filed on June 19, 1987. He was indicted for shipping 3.3. tons of cocaine into the United States, which was probably much less than he actually smuggled. It was alleged that Lehder was responsible for 80% of the cocaine loads brought into the country.

The charges covered a wide range of activities linked to drug trafficking. He was accused of importing and distributing cocaine, particularly in the United States. He was also charged with being part of a continuing criminal enterprise (CCE), which was the Medellín cartel, with close connections with other relevant names also on the DEA's list of drug lords. This belonging to a CCE implied he had been part of a long-scale criminal organization, which was a major offense.

Lehder didn't have the support of the old times, so if he wanted to walk free from this situation, he had to play with the justice laws. Thus, he and his defense tried to find a gap in the legal framework that allowed him to return to Colombia and be judged by Colombian laws.

The extradition agreement between Colombia and the United States was signed in 1979, but the Colombian government was still reluctant to accept crimes related to CCE. Moreover, the crimes Lehder was indicted for were committed between 1976 and 1980, almost all of which were prior to the agreement. However, the Colombian Supreme Court revisited the requirement and issued a favorable judgment on November 29, 1983. Lehder's first attempt to avoid justice faded.

Then, his defense presented Lehder's Motion to Enforce the Rule of Speciality and Abate Prosecution on Count XII of the Indictment and posed two different arguments. Lehder's lawyers said that the Supreme Court didn't expressly mention CCE as one of the charges that could cause extradition, even in the resolution passed in 1983. Then, they also alleged that the CCE offenses weren't specifically included in the extradition agreement signed by the two countries. Thus, Lehder's extradition was illegal since none of the cases he was charged with were labeled in the agreement.

These arguments had to be addressed by the Court in Florida. To Lehder's disappointment, his extraction was supported by the Supreme Court endorsement and a special approval signed by the president. In May 1984, the President of Colombia expressly approved Lehder's extradition. He noted (*United States v. Lehder-Rivas*, 1987):

In the past, the government had denied requests for extradition of Colombian citizens to the United States and in the respective orders has analyzed the circumstances of having so ordered and the rights which made it adopt such measures. But in the case in question, we find before us circumstances completely different, as Mr. Carlos Lehder Rivas is accused in importing cocaine to the United States, of possession of it with the intent to distribute it in North American territory and of participating in continuous criminal enterprise of narcotic traffic (para. 5).

These words were eloquent: There was no possibility for Lehder to be taken back to Colombia. If the legal framework had flaws, both countries' political motivations to keep him imprisoned were enough. Lehder's motion was irrevocably denied.

Since the legal efforts failed, Lehder made one more attempt to avoid the trial in the United States. He made a public declaration threatening to kill one federal judge every week until he was released. Soon, he realized he was no longer one of the Extraditables, and the Medellín cartel was miles away. He had lost all his power and had no choice but to accept the new circumstances.

Nonetheless, the United States Marshals took his threat very seriously. Even if Escobar had delivered him, there were no guarantees that they wouldn't come to help the old partner. After all, Lehder had information that could involve them. Thus, the Marshals provided the jury members, the judges, and the prosecutors with special bodyguards and security measures. The courthouses were constantly patrolled by guards armed with rapid-fire guns. Lehder was held inside a special cell in the courthouse while the trial was held.

## **Testimonials and Evidence During the Trial**

The trial was held between 1987 and 1988. For seven months, Judge Howell W. Melton heard the testimonials of the people who described Lehder's participation in the crimes for which he was charged and Lehder's arguments to defend himself. Outside the courthouse, the crowd gathered to witness the fall of the smuggling king. It was the first time a grand drug lord was extradited and taken to trial.

The prosecutors had plenty of evidence to prove Lehder was guilty. Among this evidence, they had photographs and videos of the planes and loads of cocaine. There were audio records of Lehder allocating the loads and establishing the routes and destinations. They even had bank transactions that proved the millionaire amounts of money Lehder had and couldn't link to any legal activity. Those proofs were irrefutable, and that was just the beginning. Direct testimonials supplied the ultimate evidence.

## **More Betrayals**

First, the prosecution brought some of Lehder's employees from Norman's Cay as witnesses. After the DEA dismantled Lehder's operation base, people who worked with him faced legal issues. They had to prove they were compelled to work for him under pressure or face charges for joining a criminal enterprise. Thus, it was easy for the prosecutors to find witnesses willing to declare against Lehder.

These witnesses provided details about the flights and the operations on the island. They talked about the parties and Lehder's frequent visitors. They explained how he used money to bribe the authorities and the neighbors and manipulated them to sell him all the properties. There was no doubt that Norman's Cay was the center of Lehder's smuggling operations and that he had corrupted the local government.

A key testimony came from a man named Carlos Toro. He was a DEA informant who worked undercover as Lehder's assistant for a while. According to his narrative, he arranged flight paths to take the drug into the United States via Florida. He was also in charge of negotiations with the distribution dealers and paid for the service to pilots and couriers. He also contributed evidence of how the Medellín cartel operated in Colombia, and later, he also provided information about the connections with Noriega, Panama's dictator (Wing, 2015).

The prosecution had a further ace up its sleeve: Jung's testimonial. Lehder's old first partner in crime had been indicted in 1985 for drug smuggling. He was sentenced to 15 years in prison. The prosecutors offered him a reduction in sentence to four years if he agreed to testify against Lehder. At first, Jung refused to do that because it was treason. However, some weeks later, as the trial advanced, the *Miami Herald* published that Lehder was willing to collaborate with the U.S. government in exchange for some benefits. Jung believed Lehder was going to accuse him and decided to take the first step (Simpson, 2020).

Jung made a phone call, and he was immediately taken to Jacksonville. He told the jury everything from the moment he met Lehder in prison when they were young, to the operations in the Bahamas, and the partnership with Escobar and the others. The prosecutors complemented the testimony with the evidence they had gathered. The jury didn't consider Lehder's lawyer, who tried to persuade the jury to dismiss Jung's testimony because he had a conflict of interest. Jung was released after testifying.

## **Justice After All**

Lehder knew that with all that evidence against him, he had no chance of being released. Thus, he made one last desperate attempt. He accused the DEA and the governments of Colombia and the United States of negotiating and paying money to the cartels in exchange for information. He also declared that the Medellín cartel had supplied the candidates for the presidential elections, and that magistrates had accepted money from drug trafficking. While this was partly true, the trial's primary purpose was to send a powerful message to society.

Until the end of the trial, Lehder continued to claim he was innocent and tried to deny his connections with the Medellín cartel. However, the weight of the evidence was overwhelming. He also tried to cling to his rights. He claimed that the CIA had been involved in his capture, which was against his individual rights, and insisted on the illegality of his extradition. Nonetheless, nothing worked. He was one of the leaders of the deadliest criminal organization, and the U.S. government would not let him go.

After hearing all the testimonies, the jury reached a verdict. Lehder was found guilty of the 11 charges for which he was indicted. He was sentenced to a life sentence plus 135 years. He was 38 years old.

## **Never Give Up**

By the time Lehder reached Florida for trial, he wasn't the smuggling king. He was over. But at least, he was free. When the Colombian police took his ranch, he couldn't imagine it was his end. Still, he received the most brutal punishment he had fought against for so long. Perhaps that was the worst defeat and humiliation: He was the first one to be extradited to the United States, the country he swore to destroy.

The sentence was the last estocade. He would spend the rest of his life behind bars. However, Carlos Lehder would not give up even in the worst circumstances. He used every resource left of his power to recover freedom and retaliate against those who betrayed him.

# CHAPTER 10
## LIFE IN PRISON AND AFTERWARD

According to modern legal systems, time in jail is meant to punish crimes and serve as an example for the rest of society. It is intended to give criminals the opportunity to make peace with the society they hurt. Even criminals deserve a second chance to reflect on their crimes and redeem themselves. However, do these principles apply to every crime? Do all criminals deserve a second chance? It is possible to believe that sentences of over 100 years don't rely too much on the hope of criminals starting a brand new life.

Lehder was condemned for many terrible crimes. Drug trafficking isn't just about making a fortune by trading illegal substances. Drugs destroy people's lives and families. Moreover, trading drugs in the most innovative ways wasn't Lehder's worst offense. He threatened people and forced them to engage in crimes, and he took part in murders and kidnappings. Can years in the shadow make a man like Lehder, persuaded of his own ideas and goals, feel remorse?

Perhaps some of this crossed through Lehder's mind. Maybe it was just his megalomania that didn't leave him, that just couldn't stand that a man with such a genius and a mission against the empire couldn't end like that. The king of the Bahamas and the whole Caribbean, the man who had the Medellín cartel in his hands, couldn't accept being a simple prisoner in a cell in the United States. That was the country that marginalized him. A cell like that was the same place where he started. His life couldn't end like that.

From day one after the sentence, Lehder devoted himself to finding a way to get out of prison. It wouldn't be an easy task because he was deprived even of the right to parole. However, he had accumulated a wide range of resources. It was just a matter of finding the correct one.

## **Struggle to Recover Freedom**

During the trial, the prosecutors and the jury made it clear that there was no chance for Lehder to be released. The trial had a massive coverage of the media, and the eyes of the world were set on what was going on in that courthouse. A man with a historical record of dozens of major crimes with tons of drugs and people murdered and tortured, even high magistrates, had to spend the rest of his life in a maximum security prison. It didn't matter if he was only one little piece of a greater monster; It had to be consistent and persuasive: Justice worked, the DEA was hunting them down, and the good guys would win the war on wars.

Lehder had these ideas clear. It wasn't just about him. He was a symbol, and while it flattered him a little, it made things much more complicated. An ordinary prisoner in his situation had relevant information to negotiate freedom, but in that context, he was the defeated villain.

Despite the disadvantageous situation, he persisted. To insist on his freedom and repatriation, Lehder relied on three main arguments:

- He was innocent because, from his own perspective, he and the other cartel members had only seen a good business opportunity and had taken it. What would anyone in his place do?
- He had been treated unfairly because extradition was illegal, and a corrupt system didn't have the moral authority to judge his actions.
- A nationalist vindication and a recall on his individual rights: He was a Colombian and deserved to die in his homeland.

Did he truly believe in his arguments? It's impossible to confirm. Carlos Lehder was always a clever proponent; every time he had a chance to address the audience, he displayed rhetorical resources and well-articulated arguments to persuade his toughest detractors. In the past, he did with the Medellín cartel members and the people working for him, he used his skills to persuade people to join his political party and support the organization, and then, he even made public declarations justifying their criminal activities. Whether he believed or not might be a mystery, but it is undeniable that time after time, he found the words and a convincing way to persuade others. In his search for freedom, it eventually worked.

### **Collaboration With the Authorities**

At first, Lehder was not requested to collaborate as an informant because it would imply benefits for him, and because the United States only wanted him in jail. Nonetheless, the situation changed when Lehder became a key witness to prove the implication in drug trafficking of a relevant figure in the political landscape. In the early 1990s, the United States was interested in showing that Manuel Noriega, the dictator president of Panama, had close connections with the Medellín cartel and had collaborated with them to smuggle drugs into the country.

Lehder knew about those connections from the inside because he was one of the prominent Medellín cartel members who negotiated with Noriega. The prosecutors carrying out the case against Noriega had circumstantial evidence, but Lehder could provide eyewitness testimonials of the negotiations, the exchange of money, and how Noriega benefited from the drug trading. The dictator had provided airstrips for the planes with drugs and protection for the traffickers to operate undisturbed.

It was an unbeatable opportunity for Lehder. He agreed to collaborate and be a witness against Noriega in exchange for a significant reduction in his 135-year sentence. It was a difficult decision for Lehder because it was still a risk to testify against powerful and dangerous people like Noriega, even while being in jail. Lehder had to enter a program of protected witnesses.

Eventually, the government of the United States agreed and offered a reduction of the sentence to 55 years and the possibility of being taken to Germany. It was less than Lehder expected, but more generous than similar situations. In 1992, Lehder appeared in court and told everything he knew about the connections between the Medellín cartel and Noriega. As a result, he got the commutation of the sentence, but nobody mentioned the option of moving to Germany. In 1995, Lehder sent a letter demanding that the rest of the agreement be fulfilled, but the answer was negative.

**Sentence Appeal**

Before appealing the sentence, Lehder found a way to make his testimony more relevant than himself as the defeated drug lord in jail. At one point, he persuaded the government that the information he could provide was significantly relevant not for his case or the Medellín cartel but for the world. However, that deserves a separate treatment in the following section. Let's first delve into the arguments Lehder displayed to obtain freedom, or at least, be taken back to his country.

Lehder appealed his sentence for the first time in 2005, when he had served about 17 years. He chose to represent himself to challenge the sentence and appeared before the U.S. Court of Appeals. According to Lehder, when indicted, he was promised to enter a collaboration program that entailed a sentence reduction, but the United States Attorney's Office refused to honor that agreement. Lehder insisted that this agreement had even considered delivering him to Germany, since he was also a German citizen. Moreover, Lehder claimed that he had been the subject of discrimination and unequal treatment for being a "Latino," labeling the act as "unconstitutional" (*Appeal From the United States District Court*, 2005).

Lehder claimed that his motion should be heard in court, but the judge rejected it as unnecessary. The arguments were that the agreement contemplated the benefits if the convict provided relevant information and proffered evidence, which Lehder had not. He had failed to prove his claims were effectively proffered, so there was no unconstitutional action to reverse (*Appeal From the United States District Court*, 2005).

After this failed attempt, Lehder shifted the strategy. In 2007, he petitioned the Supreme Court of Justice of Colombia and the President of Colombia to intervene in his case. He claimed that the extradition agreement established that the most severe sentence should not surpass 30 years, while he was condemned to 55 years after the reduction. In 2007, Lehder had already served two-thirds of the maximum sentence considered by the agreement, so he had to be released. But the Colombian government rejected his requirement.

In 2008, Carlos Lehder presented a habeas corpus petition before the Colombian Supreme Court, claiming that the government had intervened in his situation. According to Lehder, he had been extradited to the United States. The extradition treaty stipulated a maximum sentence of 20 years for extradited nationals, and his sentence was, at the time, 55 years. In 2007, Lehder fulfilled the 30 years that his conviction should have been if the treaty had been honored (*Memorandum Opinion*, 2008). Lehder insisted that it was time for him to walk free.

The judge in the case agreed and admitted that the sentence could be revisited and shortened if there was evidence that it was excessive. However, Lehder had taken so many attempts to reduce his sentence that his arguments and legal actions contradicted and overlapped, making it impossible for the judge to rule in his favor. Lehder's motion was once more denied without prejudice (*Memorandum Opinion*, 2008).

**Sensitive Approaches**

Having exhausted the formal legal paths to obtain his freedom, Lehder shifted his efforts and appealed to the human side of the President of Colombia and even that of the United States. The first attempt wasn't made by him but by his daughter, Mónica.

Between 2009 and 2012, Mónica wrote letters to the presidents of their country, first Álvaro Uribe and then Juan Manuel Santos. Mónica spoke as a daughter claiming for her father. He was getting old and his health was deteriorating, so she pleaded for mercy. The answer was always the same: The Colombian government wouldn't take any action to benefit Lehder until he asked for public apologies for his many crimes.

On his end, Lehder also wrote letters to the president asking for his intervention. Every time, he seemed to show no regret for what he had done. On the contrary, he still believed he and the cartel members even had good reasons to engage in drug trafficking. In a letter Lehder sent to President Uribe in 2015, he expressed (Cosoy, 2017):

Since 1970, in front of the global propagation of the stimulant drugs subculture, a group of paisas smugglers (from Medellín and the Coffee Axe), attending to the demand, were capable of achieving what alchemists failed to for millennia, to convert a kilo of refined leaves into a kilo of pure gold (para. 30) (author's translation).

He was almost proud of their accomplishment. He pictured it as an economic feat that was just a byproduct of the cultural environment. They had only engaged in a profitable business that, at the time, had no moral questions.

In the same letter, and then he replicated it everywhere, he claimed, "I deserve to die in Colombia." The word "deserve" reveals that he never gave up on his own ideas and interpretations of what he had done as a member of the Medellín cartel and the injustice he found in his extradition and sentence in a foreign country. Meanwhile, he continued refusing to apologize for his crimes. Perhaps it was part of his strategy. Besides his internal evaluation of his acts, if he apologized for his crimes, it implied admitting them, which could hamper his options for release.

Despite his many efforts, Lehder didn't achieve his goal. He remained in prison until 2020, after serving 33 years in the Federal Penitentiary of Marion, Illinois.

## **The Release**

Lehder was eventually released before the full sentence was fulfilled. After the reduction of 135 to 55 years of a sentence that deprived him of the right to parole, he obtained more benefits. None of the many tactics Lehder tried worked, but still, the legal system benefited him.

It was a combination of elements. Firstly, the U.S. legal system considers a reduction in the sentence for the observation of good behavior. Inmates gain 54 days of good behavior per year. In 33 years, he had nearly 5 years to discount from the total, but that wasn't enough.

On the other side, Lehder was diagnosed with prostate cancer in 2017, and his health was seriously compromised. In jail, he wouldn't have access to treatment, and he also had other chronic diseases.

His daughter Mónica never stopped looking for a way to help his father, and when she knew about his illness, she doubled her efforts.

There are no available records of the details of how Carlos Lehder achieved freedom again. According to Mónica Lehder's public declarations to the media, her father observed exemplary behavior, but his health conditions were determinant in obtaining a release based on compassionate considerations. Finally, on June 15, 2020, Lehder was set free.

Like in 1987, the U.S. Marshals escorted Carlos Lehder to take a plane. This time, instead of taking him to prison, that plane was his ticket to freedom and a new life. The flight headed to Frankfurt, Germany.

## **His Life After Prison**

Carlos Lehder's father was German, and thus, he held German citizenship. Germany agreed to allow his entrance, and his daughter awaited him. By the time Lehder reached Germany, her daughter had made connections with a non-profit organization that hosted him and committed to caring for him.

Lehder, old and ill, was ready to start a second different life. Over time, he fought and defeated cancer and lived his life as a free man. After denying his crimes for so long, he eventually expressed remorse for some of his actions. He had always enjoyed being a public person. In many of his interviews, he described feeling like a rock star when he was the smuggling king and ruled in the Caribbean. He embraced a new phase as a popular personality, and following his release, he has participated in numerous interviews.

In this new version, he has shown himself to be a reflective person and has shown remorse for his participation in drug trafficking. Even though he refused to when the Colombian president requested it, he finally apologized for his crimes. In an interview with Semana Magazine, he said that based on moral and Christian values, he looks into other citizens' eyes and asks for forgiveness because I was a member of the Medellín Cartel(Redacción Nación, 2024).

In the interviews and testimonials he gave to biographers, and also his book of memories, he eventually admitted his role as the one responsible for the delivery and distribution of the drugs traded by the Medellín cartel. He has spoken openly about how the cartel smuggled drugs into the United States and provided details about the crimes committed by the organization. Nonetheless, he continues to deny his participation in major crimes such as the murder of Lara Bonilla. For most of those crimes, Lehder insists on blaming Escobar, and to the last minute, Lehder continues to affirm it was Escobar who delivered him to the U.S. authorities.

He published a memoir titled *Vida y Muerte del Cartel de Medellín (Life and Death of the Medellín Cartel)* in August 2024. He wrote the book while in Germany. Besides admitting his crimes, he no longer talks about them with a sense of pride. Instead, he recalls those days with regret and says his performance as a smuggler was a huge mistake. He highlights that after the moment he was captured, he never again engaged in any criminal action at any time, not when he was in jail and never since he was released.

When asked about the reasons to publish a book with his memories and openly talking about his murky past, Lehder has explained that he hopes his experiences and journey would persuade others to enter the drug trade. In the prologue of his book, he wrote:

Further reflecting on his past, Lehder authored a memoir titled *Vida y muerte del cartel de Medellín*, in which he expressed his hope that his experiences would deter others from entering the drug trade. He wrote, "Hopefully, my memoirs will help new generations understand firsthand the hazardous, treacherous, and harmful path of drug trafficking. In it, there are two guarantees, with very few exceptions: one will always end up in prison or in the funeral home" (Redacción Nación, 2024, para. 3) (translation by the author).

In his book, Lehder also highlights the impact of cocaine on people's lives and society, and argues against drug trading and substance consumption. He has publicly expressed that he hopes drugs will never be legalized, except for marijuana. At present, he considers himself a contrite and rehabilitated man who deserves and is enjoying a second chance in life. He believes he has paid his debt to society.

## Back at Home

Carlos Lehder left his country in 1987 on a plane and headed to Florida. When he was released, he went directly to Germany. One day, he returned to his homeland. On March 28, 2025, Lehder landed in Bogotá. He was back at home after 38 years.

The moment he set foot on Colombian territory, he was arrested at the El Dorado Airport. The Attorney General's Office confirmed that there were no such records. On the other hand, Colombian Migration claimed that they had to check if there was any judicial record of crimes committed by Lehder in the country, or any open case filed against him. The Migration Office claimed that they had an active arrest warrant for the conviction for drug trafficking and arms trafficking in their information systems (Cohen, 2025).

Lehder's lawyer, Sondra McCollins, declared that Lehder had no records linking him to criminal proceedings. Eventually, this was confirmed, and after 48 hours in detention, Lehder was finally released. He can walk throughout Colombia as a free man with no charges pending. For the law, he started a new life from scratch and can return to Germany or remain in his homeland as he pleases.

## **Redemption**

At present, Lehder is an old man. In his speech, he reveals that he has reflected on his acts, though it is still hard to tell if he knows something like remorse. It is a man who has dealt with his own mistakes and didn't have a chance to boast about his achievements, whatever he considers them to be. His testimonials show that he still can't understand why he couldn't see the betrayal that pushed him to the United States. One day, he was a leader; overnight, he had lost it all.

Along with a balance of his struggles, triumphs, and defeats, Lehder still seems concerned about showing his innocence and noble principles. At some point, he always believed in his own revolution and was convinced that his crimes were just means to achieve a greater goal for his nation. To the last minute, after loneliness and suffering, he still felt he deserved a different ending for his life, and never stopped fighting for it. Finally, he had a last victory. He walked away free, returned to his land, and chose where to live the final years near one of the few people who truly loved him. Is he at peace? Nobody knows. But we can say he can't cause any more harm.

# CONCLUSION

When looking back at historical processes, it is common to spotlight certain characters and moments. In this sense, it is usually believed that people like Griselda Blanco, Pablo Escobar, and Carlos Lehder were responsible for the boom of drugs in the 1970s and the architects of the global drug market. While their outstanding participation can't be overlooked, giving them such credit only highlights what they did. Lehder was a central piece of that gear, the one who designed the routes and bases to trade and distribute drugs, but more than an architect, he seems to have been a clever opportunist who saw his chance and took it.

Lehder indeed multiplied exponentially the volume and profit of drug dealing. Without his strategies and recklessness in dealing with their enemies, the Medellín cartel would have been less effective. Nonetheless, when Escobar delivered him and removed him from the team, it proved that Lehder was important but not essential to the cartel. After Lehder went to jail, the cartel continued operating and became even more feared by the Colombian government and society. That must have been another strike on Lehder's megalomania and delusions of grandeur. In the end, he was just another criminal.

When revisiting lives like Lehder's, it is impossible not to wonder if he was truly evil or if the circumstances just carried him along. Once he entered the business and engaged with dangerous people, what else could he do to remain in the game and alive? Readers might have their own answers. What can't be denied is that Lehder was a key piece in turning the business into a far-reaching criminal organization. Even if he wasn't the mastermind behind the system of horror established by Escobar, Lehder was engaged in murders and thousands of indirect crimes.

He went to jail and was judged according to the most severe laws. Justice frustrated his many attempts to get freed before his sentence was fulfilled. Ultimately, he got away with it because he paid much less than half of the sentence. After all his complaints, he benefited from the law he turned his back on for such a long time. Lehder enjoyed the protection of the law and claimed his rights, even though he denied those rights to the victims of his crimes.

Lehder's extradition and his time in prison served as an example, but the impact on the war on drugs was limited. While every effort counts, it is clear that the problem is much broader than just individual names. For now, it is a light of hope that his experiences and testimonials can deter others from entering a world from which the options are to end up killed by the police or the enemies, or behind bars for life.

Lehder's story has taken us on a complex journey of exploration of human nature: greed, the search for success, lack of scruples, guilt, and remorse. It leaves open questions about how far the darker aspects of the human mind and soul can take individuals and whether, in the end, it is possible to feel redeemed and find peace.

# REFERENCES

Alsema, A. (2025, March 31). *Court orders release of Medellin Cartel founder Carlos Lehder.* Colombia Reports. Districthttps://colombiareports.com/court-orders-release-of-medellin-cartel-founder-carlos-lehder/

AP. (1984, May 1). *Justice Minister slain in Bogota.* The New York Times. https://www.nytimes.com/1984/05/01/world/justice-minister-slain-in-bogota.html

*Appeal from the United States District Court for the Middle District of Florida.* (2005, June 22). https://media.ca11.uscourts.gov/opinions/unpub/files/200414298.pdf

Bauer, P. (n.d.). Carlos Lehder. In *Encyclopedia Britannica.* Retrieved May 6, 2024. https://www.britannica.com/biography/Carlos-Lehder

Bowie, D. (2024, March 1). *The rise and fall of George Jung: The real-life subject of 'Blow'.* HowStuffWorks? https://history.howstuffworks.com/historical-figures/george-jung.htm

Britto, L. (2020, September 28). *The Drug Wars in Colombia.* Latin American History.

https://oxfordre.com/latinamericanhistory/display/10.1093/acrefore/9780199366439.001.0001/acrefore-9780199366439-e-504

Burton, M. (2019, September 27). *1960s counterculture and cannabis*. LinkedIn. https://www.linkedin.com/pulse/1960s-counterculture-cannabis-mark-burton/

*Carlos Lehder*. (n.d.). Historica Fandom. https://historica.fandom.com/wiki/Carlos_Lehder

*Carlos Lehder: Pablo Escobar's crime partner freed from US jail*. (2020, June 17). BBC. https://www.bbc.com/news/world-latin-america-53070547

*Carlos Lehder personality*. (2023, August 18). PDB. https://www.personality-database.com/profile/237168/carlos-lehder-criminals-mbti-personality-type

Catiang, P. (2018, November 18). *King of sea and sky: tracing Escobar's drug routes by the vehicles and tactics he used*. ABS CBN. https://www.abs-cbn.com/ancx/culture/spotlight/11/18/18/the-king-of-sea-and-sky

Cosoy, N. (2017, February 3). *"Mesiánico y obsesivo": así era Carlos Lehder, el primer gran narco colombiano extraditado a EE.UU. hace 30 años*. BBC. https://www.bbc.com/mundo/noticias-america-latina-38857918

County Office Law. (2025, February 2). *What were the charges against Carlos Lehder and how was he extradited to the United States?* [Video]. YouTube. https://www.youtube.com/watch?v=Ht9QBc4cFoc

Cran, W. (1997, March 25). *The godfather of cocaine.* Frontline. https://www.pbs.org/wgbh/pages/frontline/shows/drugs/archive/godfathercocaine.html

Dodd, O. (2024, April 12). Uncovering the sources of revolutionary violence: the case of Colombia's National Front (1958-1964). *Small Wars & Insurgencies, 35*(5), 865-895. https://www.tandfonline.com/doi/full/10.1080/09592318.2024.2336635#abstract

The Editors of Encyclopedia Britannica. (n.d.). War on Wars. In *Encyclopedia Britannica.* Retrieved May 8, 2024. https://www.britannica.com/topic/war-on-drugs

Emblin, R. (2025, March 31). *Carlos Lehder's sudden return to Colombia revives legacy of Medellin cartel.* The City Paper. https://thecitypaperbogota.com/news/carlos-lehders-sudden-return-to-colombia-revives-legacy-of-medellin-cartel/

*Escobar Trade Route.* (n.d.). Flightsim.to. https://es.flightsim.to/file/20197/escobar-drug-routes

Ferranti, S. (2016, January 9). *The Nazi-loving drug lord who revolutionized the cocaine smuggling industry.* Vice. https://www.vice.com/en/article/the-nazi-loving-drug-lord-who-revolutionized-the-medellin-cocaine-cartel-111/

Green, P. (n.d.). *La organización.* Cocainenomics. https://www.wsj.com/ad/cocainenomics-es

InSight Crime. (2025, February 3). *Cartel de Medellín.* Insight Crime. https://insightcrime.org/es/noticias-crimen-organizado-colombia/cartel-de-medellin/

*Interview Carlos Toro*. (n.d.). Frontline. https://www.pbs.org/wgbh/pages/frontline/shows/drugs/interviews/toro.html

*Interview George Jung*. (n.d.). Frontline. https://www.pbs.org/wgbh/pages/frontline/shows/drugs/interviews/jung.html

*It happened here*. (n.d.). United States District Court. Middle District of Florida. https://www.flmd.uscourts.gov/it-happened-here#:~:text=Former%20United%20States

Hardy, J. (1987, November 19). *Witness describes drug smuggling operation*. UPI. https://www.upi.com/Archives/1987/11/19/Witness-describes-drug-smuggling-operation/1084564296400/

Hartlyn, J. (1993). Drug trafficking and democracy in Colombia in the 1980s. ICPS. https://www.corteidh.or.cr/tablas/16400.pdf

Hernández, J.H. (2024, Enero 14). *Al descubierto la complicidad de Cuba, Panamá, Nicaragua y Bahamas con el tráfico de drogas*. Hyper Media. https://hypermediamagazine.com/actualidad-noticias-prensa-sucesos-cuba/analisis-noticias-debates-actualidad/al-descubierto-la-complicidad-de-cuba-panama-nicaragua-y-bahamas-con-el-trafico-de-drogas/

*Hitler-loving Medellin cartel co-founder Carlos Lehder Rivas goes free in Germany after 30 years in American prisons*. (n.d.). Mail Online. https://www.dailymail.co.uk/news/article-8427781/Hitler-loving-Medellin-cartel-founder-Carlos-Lehder-Rivas-goes-free-Germany.html

Lancheros, K. (2025, April 2). *Las mujeres de Carlos Lehder: quiénes fueron las compañeras de excapo del cartel de Medellín.* Infobae. https://www.infobae.com/colombia/2025/04/02/las-mujeres-de-carlos-lehder-quienes-fueron-las-companeras-de-excapo-del-cartel-de-medellin/

Lasky, J. (2023). *Medellín Cartel.* EBSCO. https://www.ebsco.com/research-starters/law/medellin-cartel

Lehder, C. (n.d.). *El día que nació el cartel de Medellín.* Lengua. https://www.penguinlibros.com/ar/revista-lengua/no-ficcion/carlos-lehder-el-dia-que-nacio-el-cartel-de-medellin?srsltid=AfmBOooCQ0gNwYo_8VCbhofFTsf9Zi4xuY8pZCtwMeVZ5BVzHn15Nj5R

Long, W. (1988, February 21). *Billionaire drug trafficker rules: Powerful Medellin Cartel safe in its Colombia base.* Los Angeles Time. https://www.latimes.com/archives/la-xpm-1988-02-21-mn-44055-story.html

Masters, J. (2020, January 8). *What is extradition?* Council of Foreign Relations. https://www.cfr.org/backgrounder/what-extradition

*Medellín cartel co-founder transferred to Germany after prison sentence.* (2020, June 16). The Guardian. https://www.theguardian.com/world/2020/jun/16/carlos-lehder-rivas-medellin-cartel-transferred-germany

*Memorandum Opinion.* (2008, June 20). United States District Court for the District of Columbia. https://www.govinfo.gov/content/pkg/USCOURTS-dcd-1_07-cv-01733/pdf/USCOURTS-dcd-1_07-cv-01733-0.pdf

*The midnight murder that threatened Pablo Escobar's empire.* (n.d.). Noiser. https://www.noiser.com/real-narcos/the-midnight-murder-that-threatened-pablo-escobars-empire

Nagle, L. (1991, June 1). The Rule of Law or the Rule of Fear: Some Thoughts on Colombian Extradition. Loyola of Los Angeles International and Comparative Law Review, 13(4). https://digitalcommons.lmu.edu/cgi/viewcontent.cgi?referer=&httpsredir=1&article=1232&context=ilr

*National Latin Movement.* (n.d.). Historica Fandom. https://historica.fandom.com/wiki/National_Latin_Movement

Newsroom Infobae. (2022, April 23). *Murder to justice: chronicle of the assassination of Rodrigo Lara Bonilla on the eve of its anniversary.* Infobae. https://www.infobae.com/en/2022/04/23/murder-to-justice-chronicle-of-the-assassination-of-rodrigo-lara-bonilla-on-the-eve-of-its-anniversary/

*Norman's Cay.* (n.d.). Historica Fandom. https://historica.fandom.com/wiki/Norman%27s_Cay

*Norman's Cay: Playground business.* (n.d.). PBS. https://www.pbs.org/wgbh/pages/frontline/shows/drugs/business/cay.html

Noticias Caracol. (2020, June 17). Carlos Lehder será tratado por cáncer de próstata en Alemania. https://www.noticiascaracol.com/colombia/carlos-lehder-sera-tratado-por-cancer-de-prostata-en-alemania

Quesada, J.D. (2024, April 15). *The truth about Carlos Lehder, Pablo Escobar's feared associate*. El País. https://english.elpais.com/international/2024-04-15/the-truth-about-carlos-lehder-pablo-escobars-feared-associate.html

Redacción Nación. (2024, January 13). *Arrepentido, Carlos Lehder, uno de los excapos más conocidos del país, lanza una sentencia: "Me opongo a la legalización de la droga, excepto la marihuana."* Semana. https://www.semana.com/politica/articulo/arrepentido-carlos-lehder-uno-de-los-excapos-mas-conocidos-del-pais-lanza-una-sentencia-me-opongo-a-la-legalizacion-de-la-droga-excepto-la-marihuana/202430/?utm_source=chatgpt.com

Rennie, D. (2025, April 20). *The rise and fall of Carlos Lehder, Pablo Escobar's right-hand man who later offered to capture him for the DEA*. ATI. https://allthatsinteresting.com/carlos-lehder

Rodriguez Parrado, J.C. (2025, April 7). *Carlos Lehder desmintió su presencia en redes sociales tras su llegada a Colombia: "No tengo nada de eso."* Infobae. https://www.infobae.com/colombia/2025/04/07/carlos-lehder-desmintio-su-presencia-en-redes-sociales-tras-su-llegada-a-colombia-no-tengo-nada-de-eso/

Rubiano, A.M., Muñoz, J.H., Estebanez, G., Sanchez, A.I. & Puyana, J.C. (2018). Drugs, violence and trauma in the Colombian context: A health care point of view of a human rights challenge. *Panamerican Journal of Trauma, Critical Care & Emergency Surgery 7*(2), 158-163. doi: 10.5005/jp-journals-10030-1218

Sanchez Cristo, J. (2024, January 18). *Exclusiva: Carlos Lehder explica por primera vez la traición de Pablo Escobar.* [Video]. YouTube. https://www.youtube.com/watch?v=J72ZXNJ8y9s

Simpson, N. (2020, September 6). *George Jung comes home.* Milford Daily News. https://www.milforddailynews.com/story/news/crime/2020/09/06/did-you-see-johnny-depp-in-blow-george-jung-infamous-cocaine-smuggler-who-inspired-biopic-returned-h/113940776/

*Timeline: America's War on Drugs.* (2207, April 2) NPR. https://www.npr.org/2007/04/02/9252490/timeline-americas-war-on-drugs

Torrado, S. (2024, January 22). *Carlos Lehder revives the ghosts of Pablo Escobar and the era of the drug lords.* El Pais. https://english.elpais.com/international/2024-01-22/carlos-lehder-revives-the-ghosts-of-pablo-escobar-and-the-era-of-the-drug-lords.html

United States v. Lehder-Rivas, 668 F. Supp. 1523 (M.D. Fla. 1987). (1987, August 31). Justia. https://law.justia.com/cases/federal/district-courts/FSupp/668/1523/1403629/

*U.S. v. Reed.* (1993, January 20). VLex. https://case-law.vlex.com/vid/u-s-v-reed-893629184

Whelan, C. (2015, January 15). *Local news biggest New York events of the 1960s.* CBS News. https://www.cbsnews.com/newyork/news/biggest-new-york-events-of-the-1960s/

Wing, N. (2015, April 9). *Devil's bargain: A former Medellin cartel official has been a DEA informant for 27 years. Now he wants out.* Huffpost. https://www.huffpost.com/entry/carlos-toro-dea-informant_n_7019466

Wing, N. (2015, September 15). DEA informant who helped defeat Medellín cartel sues feds for back pay. Huffpost. https://www.huffpost.com/entry/carlos-toro-dea-informant-lawsuit_n_55e606f2e4b0c818f619825a

www.ingramcontent.com/pod-product-compliance
Lightning Source LLC
Chambersburg PA
CBHW071210070526
44584CB00019B/2984